STEEL
GIANTS

Stephen G. McShane and Gary S. Wilk

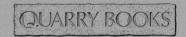

QUARRY BOOKS

AN IMPRINT OF
INDIANA UNIVERSITY PRESS
BLOOMINGTON AND INDIANAPOLIS

STEEL GIANTS

Historic Images from the Calumet Regional Archives

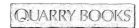

AN IMPRINT OF

INDIANA UNIVERSITY PRESS

BLOOMINGTON AND INDIANAPOLIS

This book is a publication of

Quarry Books
an imprint of
Indiana University Press
601 North Morton Street
Bloomington, IN 47404-3797 USA

http://iupress.indiana.edu

Telephone orders   800-842-6796
Fax orders   812-855-7931
Orders by e-mail   iuporder@indiana.edu

The paper used in this publication meets the
minimum requirements of American National
Standard for Information Sciences—Permanence
of Paper for Printed Library Materials,
ANSI Z39.48-1984.

Manufactured in China

Library of Congress Cataloging-in-Publication Data

McShane, Stephen G.
  Steel giants : historic images from the Calumet Regional
Archives / Stephen G. McShane and Gary S. Wilk.
      p. cm.
  Includes bibliographical references and index.
  ISBN 978-0-253-35299-6 (cloth : alk. paper) 1. Steel
industry and trade—Indiana—Calumet—History—Pictorial
works. 2. Steel industry and trade—Indiana—History—
Pictorial works. I. Wilk, Gary S. II. Title.
  HD9518.C35M35 2009
  338.4'766910977299—dc22
                                          2008037540

  3 4 5 6 18 17 16 15 14

To Cindy, Maureen, and Renée,
FOR BELIEVING, AS ALWAYS

AND

TO MY FAMILY,
Nancy, Justin, and Becky

MY PARENTS,
Dorothy and Frank

MY IN-LAWS,
Harvey and Bobbie

AND THE PAST AND PRESENT
steel employees of Inland and U.S. Steel

Contents

Workers at Madeline blast furnace no. 1, November 1907.
Inland Steel Company Indiana Harbor Works.

Acknowledgments

Many talented individuals helped us to produce *Steel Giants,* and they have our everlasting gratitude. We would like to thank, first and foremost, our families for their tireless support: Cindy, Maureen, and Reneé McShane; Nancy, Justin, Becky, Dorothy, and Frank Wilk; and Harvey and Bobbie Nagle.

This book is the culmination of a multistage, multiyear project at Indiana University Northwest entitled *Lake Michigan's Steel Shores,* which included exhibits, oral histories, digitization of historical photographs, and a web site. Our colleagues at Indiana University Northwest (IUN) assisted us in so many ways. IUN Chancellor Bruce W. Berland and the faculty, staff, students, and administration of our campus sustained us throughout the project.

Our deep appreciation goes out to Professor Neil Goodman, Chair of the Center for Cultural Discovery and Learning's Curatoriate, and to the Curatoriate members for their ceaseless enthusiasm and encouragement; to Patricia Lundberg, former executive director of the Center and her staff of Roxanne Brown, Tashena Lollis, and Victoria Brockett, along with the Center for Regional Excellence's executive director Debbie Thomas, for financial backing and project advocacy at all stages and at all levels; to Calumet Regional Archives co-directors Ronald D. Cohen and James B. Lane, without whom there would be no Archives and therefore no steel history collections; to Director of Library Services Timothy L. Sutherland and the faculty, staff, and students in the IUN library, as well as to Robert F. Moran, former IUN library director and mentor; to our IUN colleagues William Dorin, Kel Knaga, Lou Ann Karabel, Harry Karabel, Bill Allegrezza, Ann Fritz, Dave Klamen, Ken Schoon, and a number of IUN students for their many contributions to the *Lake Michigan's Steel Shores* project. We would like to offer special thanks to Peg Schoon, assistant archivist in the Calumet Regional Archives, for her research and suggestions, particularly for the book's title.

A number of people in our northwest Indiana community also played key roles in this endeavor. We are most grateful to Joseph Medellin and David C. Allen of ArcelorMittal Indiana Harbor, along with ArcelorMittal's Don Olson and Doug Houghmiller, who were responsible for ensuring the preservation of the Inland Steel Company Photograph Collection in the Calumet Regional Archives; similarly, we owe a debt of gratitude to Ed Charbonneau, Tom Ferrall, Tedd Urice, Fosty Bella, and Keith Kolb of U.S.

Steel's Gary Works, for their efforts to place historical photographs and other materials from the Gary plant in the Archives. Our colleagues at Purdue University Calumet, especially Lance Trusty, Rebecca House, and Katherine Carpenter played important roles in securing the Archives' collections. Paul Myers, Archibald McKinlay, Jason Lindquist, Bob Meyers, Janet Moran, and Lauren Rhein also provided valuable assistance.

We very much appreciate the hard work of the folks at Indiana University Press and Quarry Books, especially Linda Oblack, Jan Jenkins, Bob Sloan, and Brian Herrmann.

Last but not least, we would like to extend heartfelt thanks to the past and present steel workers at Gary Works and Indiana Harbor Works, and to the photographers who captured their steel-making on film. For without them, these wonderful historical images would not exist.

Stephen G. McShane
Gary S. Wilk
Indiana University Northwest
May 2009

Foreword

They came as armies, men who marched through clock-house gates into half-opened sheds and across sprawling docks along the southern tip of Lake Michigan. At first glimpse, the scene resembled nothing so much as Dante's vision of Hell. Smoke poured from a thousand stacks. Fire spat out of dark corners. Red-hot ingots, standing upright on flatcars and glowing like jack-o-lanterns, darted between buildings, pulled by straining locomotives. Blast furnaces dotted the area like the burned stumps of a giant forest.

From 1896 to 1970, the United States was the largest producer of steel in the world. Steelmaking was not only this country's biggest business in its heyday; it was also a peculiarly American one, embodying a sense of supersized sprawl, of intense and full-throttled power, that characterized our culture of abundance. This quality of magnitude reached its apotheosis along 16 miles of shoreline between Gary and the Illinois state line. Here was a place where tens of thousands of Indiana residents sweated and strained to turn gritty lumps of iron ore into skyscraper beams, ship hulls, and other products useful to man.

Steel Giants is a pictorial history of that world, concentrating on the period between 1906 and the 1960s, the golden age of steel-making in the region. The photographs were selected by Stephen G. McShane and Gary S. Wilk from two collections preserved in the Calumet Regional Archives: the U.S. Steel Gary Works Photograph Collection and the Inland Steel Company Photograph Collection. The photos are organized into chapters that show the building of the mills, the processes by which steel was made, the growth of the cities of Gary and Indiana Harbor, and the daily lives of steelworkers.

Some background may be useful to understand how Indiana fit into the industry's history. Commercial-scale steelmaking did not get underway in this country until after the Civil War, a full decade after Britain's Henry Bessemer developed an efficient method of ridding iron of its chief impurity, carbon. Iron contains about 3 percent carbon; in steel, carbon is nearly always under 1 percent and often as little as 0.05 percent.

"Decarburization" made steel both stronger and more malleable than iron, heretofore the chief building block of railroads, bridge structures, and machinery. Tests showed that a Bessemer steel rail could last up to twenty times longer than an iron rail. Not surprisingly, it was the railroads that first bankrolled the Bessemer mills that sprang up in eastern Pennsylvania and around Pittsburgh after 1867. Over the next two decades, the industry grew exponentially, producing 4.8 million tons of steel in 1890, compared to less than 80,000 tons in 1870.

This blistering pace of expansion was achieved not only through the adoption of new technology (most notably, the Siemens-Martin, or open hearth, furnace), but from radical changes in labor relations. In the old furnaces and foundries, skilled ironmongers held sway over the pace of production. Many of them were members of the Amalgamated Iron Workers or sister organizations. The Bessemer railmakers put a stop to the union shop by hiring immigrants and "buckwheats" (country boys) and placing them on 12-hour-a-day shifts. When the shifts changed on Sundays, one crew was given the day off, while the other crew was placed on duty for 24 hours straight, typically from 7 AM Sunday until 7 AM Monday.

The same companies pioneered "integrated" manufacturing, placing the different stages of production—the distillation of coke from coal, the smelting of iron from ore, the refinement of coking coal, the production of iron, the refinement of iron to steel, and the rolling of steel into finished shapes—into one centralized location. So different was this kind of business model that a new word was needed to describe it. Terms like "factory" and "mill" seemed wholly inadequate to account for the agglomeration of materials and equipment at places like Homestead, Pennsylvania. "Factory" implied a single building or a discrete unit of manufacturing, while "mill" originated from agricultural activities. Soon a word crept into the popular vocabulary that captured this new industrial form by pinpointing the overriding function of its interlocked buildings and moving conveyances—"the works."

Demands by railroads and farm-equipment producers drew railmakers to the Midwest and simultaneously encouraged them to widen their product base. In 1889, the Illinois Steel Company consolidated ownership of Chicago steelmaking and expanded its property on the city's south side. The "South Works" signaled Chicago's arrival as a major steel center. The subsequent discovery of iron ore on the Mesabi Range north of Duluth, Minnesota, only increased the city's strategic advantage. In 1895, the world's largest open-pit mine, the Hull-Rust-Mahoning mine, was opened, permitting the economic shipment of ore via a rail link to Duluth and water transport on the Great Lakes. With its access to deep water and close proximity to the Windy City,

Indiana's Lake County/Calumet district became irresistible to industry. "Suddenly," McShane and Wilk write, "the region became part of the nation's rapid industrialization."

The transformation of northwest Indiana from a lonely and unsettled "wasteland" (a term used repeatedly by contemporaries) into a manufacturing behemoth is described by McShane and Wilk in the introduction. Suffice it to say that Inland Steel first entered the steel industry in 1893, establishing a small plant in Chicago Heights, a Chicago suburb. What followed was a much larger facility, started in 1901, directly on Lake Michigan, called Indiana Harbor Works. When U.S. Steel decided to erect its own works east of Indiana Harbor in 1905, the region's fate was sealed. The Gary Works (named after U.S. Steel Chairman Elbert H. Gary) became the showcase of the world's then-largest corporation. Supplemented by a plant erected by the Mark Manufacturing Company (later Youngstown Sheet and Tube at East Chicago), steel became the leading industry in Indiana, with output valued at $333 million in 1929.

On the national stage, the Lake Michigan District took on increased importance after the Great Depression. Including the mills across the border in Illinois, the region made 20 million ingot tons of steel in 1944. Its output had edged out production in the Eastern District anchored in eastern Pennsylvania and Maryland and was second only to Pittsburgh–Youngstown, cradle of the original industry. Together, the three districts made 40 percent of the world's steel in the 1950s, reassuring Cold War commentators that America was maintaining a wide margin of economic superiority over the Soviet Union and the newly formed People's Republic of China.

———————

From its opening in 1909, the Gary Works was writ large, the greatest manufacturer of iron and steel on the globe, a title it did not surrender until 1958, when it was surpassed for a few years by Bethlehem Steel's Sparrows Point, Maryland, works. Indiana Harbor grew more organically, in keeping with the relatively smaller capital resources of the Block family, which controlled the company's stock and management, but the works followed the same lockstep pattern of Gary. Raw materials were assembled in massive conical heaps along the shorefront; rolling shops were built in the right geometrical relation to one another; open hearths and Bessemer converters were operated on three levels simultaneously: overhead on crane ways, on the main "charging" floor, and in the basement where molten steel was teemed into ingot moulds.

Such around-the-clock activity required enormous pools of labor. Immigrants attracted by thousands of new jobs poured into northwest Indiana. Because there were no towns close by, towns had to be built. Inland constructed housing for its supervisors, but let private developers do the rest, resulting in a dingy residential district that was sandwiched between the works and East Chicago. Gary was a different story. U.S. Steel purchased 800 acres south of the mill and constructed a model community. An orderly grid of civic buildings, schools, shops, and houses arose from once-barren dunes on a system of well-planned boulevards.

But even the trainloads of topsoil that were spread across the city of Gary by the corporation could not conceal the medieval labor practices that lay inside the mills. Elbert Gary was fiercely anti-union and adamant that workers follow the practice of twelve-hour workdays, leading Carl Sandburg to pen his 1915 poem "The Mayor of Gary":

> I asked the Mayor of Gary about the 12-hour day
>   and the 7-day week.
> And the Mayor of Gary answered more workmen steal
>   time on the job in Gary than any other place in
>   the United States.
> "Go into the plants and you will see men sitting
>   around doing nothing—machinery does everything,"
>   said the Mayor of Gary . . .
> And I said good-bye to the Mayor of Gary and I went
>   out from the city hall and turned the corner
>   into Broadway.
> And I saw workmen wearing leather shoes scruffed
>   with fire and cinders, and pitted with little holes
>   from running molten steel,
> And some had bunches of specialized muscles around
>   their shoulder blades hard as pig iron, muscles
>   of their forearms were sheet steel and they looked
>   to me like men who had been somewhere.

Pent-up anger over the 12-hour day erupted in the Great Steel Strike of 1919, when Gary became front-page news. General Leonard Wood and 1,500 U.S. troops were called to the city to restore order, and, based on later evidence, to intimidate workers. The strikers returned to work in January 1920 without a single concession made by the company, but the strike had highlighted the evils of the 12-hour day and 24-hour swing shift. President Warren Harding appealed to Gary to reduce hours as a humanitarian gesture. Gary refused. Public condemnation increased, and in 1923, Gary and other steel executives agreed to end the 24-hour swing shift and institute an 8-hour day and 6-day week "as soon as the labor supply permitted." With demand roaring, many crews continued on 7-day weeks.

Gary's death in 1927 and the stock market crash of 1929 led to a new generation of managers who agreed, under pressure from the Roosevelt administration, to sign a contract with the Steelworkers Organizing Committee (SWOC) in 1937. Inland Steel balked and joined several other companies, known collectively as "Little Steel," to fight the union. On Memorial Day 1937, gunfire by Chicago police killed ten people during a strike at the Republic Steel Works. The "Memorial Day Massacre" sent shock waves across northwest Indiana and rekindled the union effort. Inland soon recognized SWOC. In 1942, SWOC was renamed the United Steelworkers of America (USWA).

Steel remained one of Indiana's leading economic sectors through the 1960s, with more than 100,000 households tied directly or indirectly to the industry. Indeed, when Bethlehem Steel opened a new integrated works at Burns Harbor in 1964, the industry's future seemed secure. But the playing field was changing. Aluminum, concrete, and plastics began to undercut steel in some consumer and construction markets. Highly efficient when operating at full tilt, the steel giants were neither flexible nor especially economical when production started to dip. The industry was particularly unprepared for "mini-mills" that used efficient electric-arc furnaces to produce steel from scrap rather than from basic raw materials. The integrated industry needed to strike out in new directions, either by improving their product lines or lowering their prices on standard items. Instead, Big Steel responded by raising prices and blaming imports, lobbying Congress for steel quotas and other protections.

During the late 1970s and early 1980s, the industry suffered a nervous breakdown. In 1982 alone, integrated steelmakers lost $3.2 billion. Older works in Pittsburgh, Youngstown, and Chicago were closed, followed by cutbacks at mills along Lake Erie, in western New York State, across central and eastern Pennsylvania, and in Maryland. Whole communities underwent agonizing cycles of mass layoffs, resulting in only 142,000 jobs in the industry in 2001, compared to 521,000 jobs in 1974.

Northwest Indiana fared relatively well during these sad years. Bolstered by low raw-material costs and specialization as makers of automotive-grade steels, the major mills in northwest Indiana remained in operation. Inland Steel shed its independence in 1998, and Indiana Harbor Works was purchased by a predecessor of today's ArcelorMittal. The Burns Harbor and East Chicago works also became part of ArcelorMittal following the bankruptcy of their parent companies. Only the Gary Works remained under the same corporate ownership that established it.

The steel business today is vastly different from the industry depicted on the following pages. It is more decentralized in terms of production, thanks to the growth of mini-mills in the South and Southwest, and more global in terms of ownership, thanks to the entry of multinational corporations like ArcelorMittal. A great deal of modern technology has been installed at Gary and Indiana Harbor, including continuous casters and computerized rolling mills. But the future of these operations is anything but secure. In steel's biggest current market, auto manufacturing, the growth of international supply chains enables auto multinationals to import finished steel-intensive components for local assembly. And competition from substitute products has not abated; look at the growth of plastic components in household products, such as plastic microwaveable containers in place of steel cans.

The era of the steel giants is over. But the effects of an industry that pulled tens of thousands of people to northwest Indiana and shaped their lives over the course of a century can be seen in the well-planned boulevards of Gary and in the craggy black furnaces facing Lake Michigan that still make rivers of molten metal from fire and earth.

Mark Reutter
October 2008

Figure Intro.1. Inland Steel Company, East Chicago, Indiana, 1959

INTRODUCTION

Northwest Indiana's Steel Giants

OVER THE COURSE OF TWO CENTURIES, northwest Indiana became the premier steelmaking capital of the United States and often led the world in producing the metal which served, and still serves, as the backbone of industrial and economic development. It was simply a matter of the right circumstances coming together at the right time in human history, forging this small corner of the Hoosier state into a land lit at night with glowing blast furnaces and a workforce numbering in the tens of thousands. These steelworkers tamed mammoth ladles of molten iron and steel, transforming them into millions of tons of one of the strongest substances on earth. From the nineteenth century through the twentieth and into the twenty-first, the southern shores of Lake Michigan were the home of northwest Indiana's steel giants, attracting five major steel companies to build along Indiana's northern coastline.

Northwest Indiana had been home to Native American tribes and later to pioneers pushing into the region as part of the great westward movement throughout the United States. The area became known as a rich agricultural producer, particularly in the central and southern portions of Lake and Porter counties. In the mid-nineteenth century, as railroads pushed through the region on their way to Chicago, a number of small towns appeared, populated by settlers seeking a new life, railroad workers, small manufacturers, and entrepreneurs. The northern part of the region, along the Lake Michigan shoreline, served as a center of fishing, camping, and other recreational pursuits, while including several railroad towns, from Miller to Whiting. Much of northern Lake County, however, continued to be Indiana's last frontier until the latter part of the century.

The relative quiet of the dunelands ended abruptly when industrialists discovered northwest Indiana. Its plentiful and cheap land, transportation network, abundant sources of water, low taxes, a large pool of labor in neighboring Chicago, and proximity to the insatiable appetite of Midwest markets for steel during the height of America's industrial revolution, drew the industrial titans to the region. Suddenly, the region became part of the nation's rapid industrialization.

John D. Rockefeller led the charge in 1889, as Standard Oil began constructing its massive refinery in Whiting, located in the northern portion of Lake County. A dozen years later, Inland Steel Company, formed in 1893 in Chicago, became the first steelmaker in the region and in 1901 built the massive Indiana Harbor Works in East Chicago. Soon after, United States Steel Corporation arrived, breaking ground in 1906, just to the east of Indiana Harbor. U.S. Steel rapidly built a state-of-the-art steel works and a company town, naming it after U.S. Steel chairman Elbert H. Gary. As the first heats of steel were tapped in northwest Indiana, they acted as a magnet, attracting thousands of immigrants from southern and eastern Europe, filled with hope that a steel job in a steel town would lead to a better life. In the first decades of the twentieth century, the majority of the populations in these towns was foreign-born.

That ethnic "mixing bowl" characteristic of the Calumet region continued, although, as World War I broke out in Europe, the flow of European immigrants to the region was significantly reduced, just when the area's steelmakers received a flood tide of orders for war material. To alleviate the labor shortage, the industries recruited African Americans from the American south and Latinos from the southwest and south of the border to join the earlier arrivals. In the words of historian Powell Moore, "The movement of the population groups in the region during the first fifty years was such that each had the opportunity to make its presence felt. The presence of so many nationalities and races produced a variety of flavors almost unique to the Calumet Region."

In 1914, another steel plant appeared in East Chicago. Industrialist Clayton Mark established the Mark Manufacturing Company, just west of Inland Steel's Indiana Harbor Works. In addition, Mr. Mark created the first company housing in East Chicago for his employees, naming it Marks, later known as Marktown. In 1923, the American Sheet and Tube Company in East Chicago absorbed Mark Manufacturing and became Youngstown Sheet and Tube Company. Sixty years after Inland led the way, neighboring Porter County produced its own steel shores, as National Steel Corporation built its Midwest Steel plant in Portage and Bethlehem Steel constructed the last integrated steel mill in the nation at Burns Harbor.

Over the course of the twentieth century, the steel giants of northwest Indiana produced record amounts of steel. Employment surpassed 70,000 as the five plants expanded over seven decades. Although steelworkers' early efforts at unionizing were met with swift and determined resistance by management at both Inland and U.S. Steel (particularly at Gary Works during the Great Steel Strike of 1919 and at Inland during the Little Steel Strike of 1937), after World War II the United Steelworkers of America wielded enough power to wage a rash of steel strikes between 1946 and 1959. The union locals created an "industrial democracy," as historian Lance Trusty has called it, winning ever greater wages and benefits and improving the lifestyles of its members. The steel towns of East Chicago and Gary grew rapidly; some boosters proclaimed that Gary's census total by the year 2000 would exceed half a million.

And then the bottom fell out. In the 1950s, foreign imports of low-priced steel entered the U.S. market. By the 1970s, imports increasingly began to seriously cut into the market share of American steel companies. Simultaneously, domestic "mini-mills" began producing steel products without incurring the production costs of the larger integrated mills. The competition proved to be too much. During the 1980s, northwest Indiana lost more than 35,000 steel jobs, as the plants downsized, closed mills, reduced costs, and automated their operations. Inland's employment peaked at 24,000 in 1979—by 1992, the number shrank to 11,000. Gary Works' employment peaked at 26,700 in 1981; by 1992, its workforce totaled 7,850. With jobs gone and mills shrinking, the steel towns suffered numbing devastation. The populations of East Chicago and Gary peaked in 1960 at 57,669 and 178,326, respectively. By the year 2000, East Chicago's number had dwindled to 32,414, while Gary's sank to 102,746.

Ironically, by the 1990s and into the twenty-first century, the region continued as the steelmaking capital of the nation, but it needed fewer workers to keep that distinction. All five steel complexes remain in northwest Indiana today, albeit under some different names and combinations. The plants formerly known as Inland Steel and Youngstown Steel in East Chicago combined into ArcelorMittal Indiana Harbor; Bethlehem Steel in Burns Harbor is now ArcelorMittal Burns Harbor. U.S. Steel continues to operate its Gary Works, and the corporation has added neighboring Midwest Steel to its subsidiaries. Beta Steel, a mini-mill in Portage established in 1992, continues to be a viable steel producer.

In the early twentieth century, however, when only two steelmakers existed in the Calumet region of northwest Indiana, the future looked very bright. As they erected steelmaking complexes and gave rise to modern cities, Inland Steel Company and U.S. Steel's Gary Works pursued another activity: they photographed themselves. While work crews poured concrete for blast furnaces, leveled miles of dune shoreline, and tamed huge ladles of liquid iron and steel, company photographers (either in-house or contractors) captured in great detail the laborious process of building heavy industrial plants and producing record numbers of tons of steel. In essence, the two companies left behind a visual documentary record.

Fortunately, Indiana University Northwest's Calumet Regional Archives has preserved a portion of the photographic documentary record in two collections donated by these steel giants. The U.S. Steel Gary Works Photograph Collection and the Inland Steel Company Photograph Collection comprise thousands of images depicting the building and operating of the Indiana Harbor Works and the Gary Works steel plants. In addition, the collections include series of photographs of company-built sections of East Chicago and Gary. A selection of these images has been gathered together in this book.

Steel Giants and Their Steel Towns, 1901–1956: A Brief History

The year 1901 proved to be a significant one in the history of Northwest Indiana's Calumet region. On February 25, a new type of business incorporated in New Jersey. Financed by John Pierpont Morgan and directed by Elbert H. Gary, the United States Steel Corporation served as the nation's first billion dollar corporation, with authorized capital of $1,400,000,000. The Corporation, as it became known, consolidated 213 steel mills, 41 iron ore mines, a 112-oreboat fleet, and 57,000 acres of raw mate-

rial sources into one centralized entity to organize resources and facilities for maximum efficiency. Thus, from its headquarters in New York, U.S. Steel could control all aspects of production, from iron and coal mines to steel plants to railroad networks to lake shipping. With this philosophy and structure, the U.S. Steel Corporation led the steel industry at the turn of the century.

About a month later, on March 26, 1901, a special meeting of the Inland Steel Company Board of Directors convened to consider an offer by the Lake Michigan Land Company of East Chicago, Indiana. The real estate firm had offered fifty acres, free of charge, to any concern willing to invest $1,000,000 to erect an open hearth steel plant at its Indiana Harbor site in northwest Indiana. The Land Company sweetened the deal with a number of other incentives, among them the construction of a harbor for oreboats, a belt line railroad with connections to a half-dozen Chicago-area railroads, and a town near the plant site, complete with hotel, boarding house, and fifty houses (all promises were kept, including the Indiana Harbor Ship Canal and the Indiana Harbor Belt Railroad). The directors voted to accept the offer, giving birth to the region's first steel giant. The second steel giant would arrive, with much fanfare, five years later. Together, they would steel a region and a nation during the first half of the new century.

Inland Steel: A Family Company

The Inland Steel Company began by taking a chance during the worst economic downturn in U.S. history. The Panic of 1893 saw the bankruptcy of numerous business enterprises, including a steel rolling firm in the Chicago area. Established twenty years earlier, the Chicago Steel Works split old rails and rerolled them into various farm implements. The firm did well and had plans to relocate from the city to a six-acre site in Chicago Heights, Illinois. The Panic, however, put an end to those plans, as the Chicago Steel Works failed. Later that year, several employees of the Works partnered with some investors to undertake a new business venture. Those investors included Joseph Block and his son Philip D. Block, of the Block-Pollack Company of Cincinnati, Ohio. The Blocks supplied old railroad equipment to a number of companies, including the Chicago Steel Works. On October 24, 1893, the Blocks and six other investors organized the Inland

Figure Intro.2. U.S. Steel Gary Works, Gary, Indiana, 1950

Steel Company, which incorporated on October 30. Inland purchased the equipment and the Chicago Heights land contract for $8,800 (the contract also included an allowance for buildings at the site).

Construction at Chicago Heights began in November and included installing the old equipment from the defunct Chicago Steel Works. The plant started production on January 16, 1894. Old rails were heated, split, and rerolled into various agricultural implements. A secondary product line focused on manufacturing light rails for bed frames. Inland declared a profit in its first full year of operations. Four years later, Philip D. Block's older brother, Leopold E. Block, joined the firm. Their younger brother, Emanuel J. Block (called E.J. or Jimmie) came aboard in 1901, the same year Inland received an offer from a place in northwest Indiana called Indiana Harbor.

The Calumet Region of Northwest Indiana—a.k.a. Indiana's Last Frontier

Northwest Indiana was the last place to be settled in the nineteenth state. The area bordering the southern tip of Lake Michigan was inhospitable, with plentiful swamplands, sand hills, sloughs, and bitterly cold winds coming off the lake. John Tipton, a Hoosier land speculator, Indian agent, and office holder, surveyed the region in 1821 (five years after statehood) and came away unimpressed. He predicted that "the region could never be settled and that it would never be of any value to the state."

Tipton's assessment proved to be incorrect. By 1836, the Indiana General Assembly organized Porter County, followed by Lake County a year later. The county seats of Valparaiso and Crown Point sprang to life and served as focal points for development. Other small towns appeared in the area, such as Chesterton, Hobart, Cedar Lake, and St. John. A number of railroads pushed across the region in the 1850s on their way to Chicago, leading to the establishment of additional communities. Agriculture provided the economic base of the region. In 1869, George H. Hammond, Marcus M. Towle, Caleb Ives, and George W. Plumer founded the State Line Slaughterhouse (seeking to become Chicago's fourth large meatpacker) on the Indiana-Illinois border; Towle later founded the City of Hammond, Indiana, which eventually became one of the region's largest cities. Virtually all

of this development, however, occurred south of the sands and swamps along the Lake Michigan shoreline.

East Chicago, Indiana: A Twin City

If northern Lake County was viewed as isolated and unattractive, the area to become East Chicago/Indiana Harbor was the frontier within the state's last frontier. In Powell Moore's words, "This section, on the whole, was more desolate and inaccessible than any other portion of the Calumet Region." Despite its forbidding nature, the area attracted the interest of several groups of investors interested in its development. In a series of land deals between 1881 and 1887, two real estate companies, the Standard Steel and Iron Company and the Calumet Canal and Improvement Company, became the owners of the land destined to become East Chicago, Indiana, platting the site in 1887. The developers tied the east-west streets to the Chicago street numbering system to complement the name of the town and attract buyers by using the Chicago connections. In 1889, as construction began on the neighboring Standard Oil refinery in Whiting, East Chicago petitioned to become a town. In 1893, East Chicago incorporated as a city, the same year as the founding of Inland Steel Company.

While the western portion of the city developed, the east side awaited attention. In 1895, a group of Chicago investors, including Owen Aldis, Potter Palmer, and Albert De Wolfe Erskine organized the Lake Michigan Land Company. This real estate firm started purchasing lands in the eastern portion of the city from the Calumet Canal and Improvement Company and the Standard Steel and Iron Company, assigning the name Indiana Harbor to its eastern holdings. Six years later, the Lake Michigan Land Company made the offer of fifty free acres to the Inland Steel Company in 1901. That same year, a newly created real estate firm, the East Chicago Company, absorbed the Lake Michigan Land Company and began developing in earnest the Indiana Harbor section of East Chicago. It also began work on an outer harbor in Lake Michigan as part of a larger project called the Indiana Harbor Ship Canal.

Concepts for a harbor and canal in the Indiana Harbor area date back to the 1850s. As the Calumet Canal and Improvement Company began developing East Chicago, work began on dig-

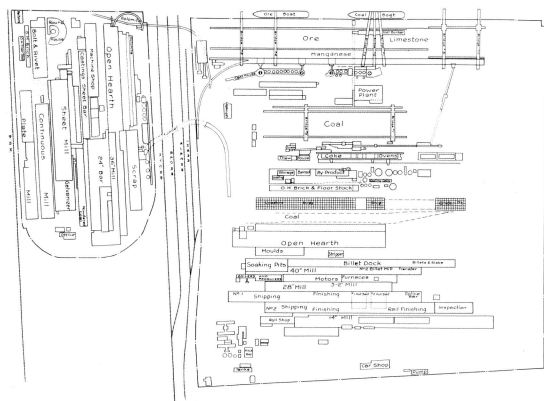

FIG. 1—Plan of plants—No. 1 plant on left

time engaged in the sale of scrap iron and steel in Pittsburgh. This business he gave up and, with his brother, P. D. Block, and others, purchased a rolling mill at Chicago Heights; which was, in 1893, incorporated as the Inland Steel Company. The officers of

Entrance plant No. 1

the Inland Steel Company when it was organized were: G. H. Jones, president; R. J. Beatty, L. E. Block and P. D. Block, vice presidents. In 1906 A. W. Thompson succeeded Mr. Jones as president, and in 1919 P. D. Block took the office. The chairmanship was created in 1919.

In charge of the several plants are:

Indiana Harbor—J. H. Walsh, general superintendent; Wilfred Sykes, assistant general superintendent.

Chicago Heights—C. B. Murton, general superintendent.

Milwaukee—E. G. Jones, general superintendent.

A financial statement issued by the Company shows that there have been issued $30,000,000 of 4½ per cent first mortgage bonds, and 12,000,000 shares of common stock paying a dividend of $3.50 a share. The profits for the first nine months of 1929 were $9,293,117.28; in the year 1928 the profits were $9,334,297.26.

Indiana Harbor Plants

The principal manufacturing units of the Inland Steel Company are located at Indiana Harbor and are designated by the company as Plants No. 1 and No. 2. Other smaller units are at Chicago Heights, Ill. and Milwaukee, Wis. Indiana Harbor lies about 20 miles east of Chicago on the southern shore of Lake Michigan.

Plant No. 1 is the older of the two Indiana Harbor units, as it was here in 1901 that the company first broke ground. Within the fences of this plant there are 52 acres of ground on which are 12 open-hearth furnaces, a 36-in. blooming mill, a sheet bar mill, a billet mill, a 24-in. bar mill, a sheet mill, a plate mill, a bolt and rivet shop, and a continuous bar mill. These departments, as will be noticed by reference to Fig. 1, ging a canal but ceased shortly afterward. The Lake Michigan Land Company/East Chicago Company resurrected the project in 1901, completing the outer harbor two years later. It included a northern breakwater extending 1,800 feet into Lake Michigan, along with a 1,200-foot southern breakwater. In October 1903, three thousand people witnessed Indiana governor Winfield T. Durbin pressing an electric button to start the dredges for the ship canal. By 1907, the first section of the canal was completed in time for delivery of raw materials for steelmaking to the Inland Steel docks on the south side of the canal. By 1925, the canal was completed and deeded to the federal government for oversight and maintenance. Dredged to a depth of twenty-two feet to accommodate oceangoing vessels, the canal's main branch extended from the outer harbor in Lake Michigan, southwesterly two miles, to a junction called "the forks." One fork extended south to connect with the Grand Calumet River. The other fork extended west toward Hammond.

A variety of industries, from metals to oil to other manufacturers, set up along the main channel and both forks of the ship canal. In 1927, the East Chicago Dock Terminal Company constructed docks, railroad tracks, cranes, and other equipment at the forks of the canal to load and unload cargo. It also included rail lines connected to a number of Chicago-area railroads. With this improvement, industries not located directly on the canal could use it for shipping. The waterway soon became one of the busiest on the Great Lakes, moving 875,306 tons of cargo in 1922 to 5,287,760 tons in 1929. The first foreign ship entered the canal in 1928, carrying a special type of pig iron from England.

While the Indiana Harbor Ship Canal attracted many industries and became a boon to the economy of East Chicago (and the Calumet region, as well as the state of Indiana), it also sliced the city into two pieces, resulting in the nickname Twin City. Indeed, for a number of years, the two sections developed independent cultures and identities, since no convenient route existed to travel between them. Although the twins both resided under the municipal jurisdiction of the City of East Chicago, the western section became known as East Chicago, and the eastern portion as Indiana Harbor.

The First Giant Arrives: The Indiana Harbor Works

After Inland Steel's directors accepted the Lake Michigan Land Company's offer in 1901, Leopold E. Block visited the site on the lakefront of Indiana Harbor. He discovered that twenty of the fifty free acres awarded to the company lay under water. Nevertheless, design and construction got underway. Inland planned to build four open hearth furnaces, a blooming mill, and a bar mill in Indiana Harbor. Because the plant's designers were familiar with manufacturing steel sheet, sheet mills were added to the project. On July 21, 1902, the Inland Steel Company poured the first steel ingot in northern/northwest Indiana.

By 1905, the four open hearth furnaces produced sixteen to eighteen heats of steel per week. The plant included a bar mill, blooming mill, seven sheet mills, gas plant, machine shop, pipe shop, blacksmith shop, and laboratory. What it lacked, however, was a blast furnace to make its own pig iron; the company had chosen instead to import its pig iron by rail. In 1906, Inland decided to convert its Indiana Harbor Works into an integrated steel mill, controlling raw materials acquisition and producing its own pig iron. The company purchased the Laura Mine in Minnesota's Mesabi iron range and commenced building a blast furnace, expanding on landfill into Lake Michigan and calling the addition Plant 2. On July 29, 1907, the oreboat *M.A. Hanna* delivered the first load of iron ore to the new Inland Steel docks on the Indiana Harbor Ship Canal. On August 31, five-year-old Madeline Block, daughter of Philip D. Block, lit the Madeline No. 1 blast furnace (Madeline would light a total of seven blast furnaces at Indiana Harbor Works between 1907 and 1980), manufacturing the first pig iron in Indiana.

During its first half century, Inland's Indiana Harbor Works expanded continuously. The Plant 2 peninsula grew to more than 700 acres by 1951. Expansion programs during the First World War added more open hearth furnaces, blast furnaces, coke ovens, sheet mills, galvanizing lines, and a bolt and rivet plant. The company established a fleet of ore carriers, along with coal and iron ore mines. Hard times during the Great Depression failed to deter expansion, as hot strip and cold rolling mills were added, as well as the nation's first continuous sheet and bar mills. The Second World War saw even more expansion, with the addition of Plants 3 and 4 to manufacture numerous products to wage war. Fifty years after its founding, the Indiana Harbor Works' ingot capacity totaled 3,750,000 tons, with a labor force of 18,000. In 1952, L. E. Block commented, "We didn't know that we would grow so big."

Indiana Harbor: The Twentieth Century Wonder

In the same time period, Indiana Harbor's growth rivaled that of its steel giant. Interestingly, the town was not a "company town" in the classic sense of a company building the city and constructing home sites for its workers. Certainly Inland Steel was the Twin City's largest employer and taxpayer and funded a number of civic projects; yet, Inland's only company-produced housing was the Sunnyside addition to Indiana Harbor, where in 1920, the company built a hundred duplex homes for its supervisory personnel. Instead, East Chicago/Indiana Harbor could be called a "companies town," with more than fifty distinct industries packed into a city encompassing slightly over eleven square miles—and many of those factories located in the Indiana Harbor section.

As Inland Steel broke ground for Harbor Works, the East Chicago Company wasted no time in developing the accompanying town site and attracting buyers, both industrial and residential. The Company platted 4,000 lots, installed sewers and utilities, macadamized streets, planted trees, and set aside lands for parks and for lakefront housing (mansions sprang up on the lakefront strip, owned by Inland executives and other prominent citizens). By 1904, almost 600 residences and businesses were up and running. In the words of author Archibald McKinlay, "Indiana Harbor went up like a Hollywood set." Boosters called Indiana Harbor the "Twentieth Century Wonder."

News of these developments spread quickly throughout the nation and the world. Entrepreneurs, engineers, skilled workers, and unskilled laborers poured into the city. Huge numbers of immigrants from southern and eastern Europe came to the re-

gion during this period to join earlier immigrants from northern and western Europe as well as native-born Americans. Almost overnight, tents, shacks, boarding houses, and boxcars sprung up to house these waves of newcomers cheaply. Other than the Marktown and Sunnyside housing developments, East Chicago's industries ignored their workers' housing problems. As Moore observed, "Housing for the common laborer in East Chicago was probably the worst in the Calumet Region." Skilled and semi-skilled workers settled on Block and Pennsylvania avenues near the steel plant, while new immigrants created a "Hunkytown" around Cedar Street. Gambling dens and saloons kept the residents busy. By 1910, more than 110 saloons called the Twin City home. The population numbers surged: 3,411 in 1900, 19,098 in 1910, 35,967 in 1920, and 54,784 by 1930. The 1910 census also showed another trend: more than 53 percent of East Chicago's residents were foreign-born.

The year 1906, however, saw significant change in Indiana Harbor's neighborhoods, caused by, according to McKinlay, the start of construction of U.S. Steel's Gary Works and the city of Gary to the east. Part of that project involved relocating rail lines in the area, resulting in the Baltimore & Ohio railroad redirecting its Indiana Harbor tracks right through the lakefront mansion strip. Thus, the resort-like atmosphere disappeared, as the homeowners either moved their mansions or tore them down. Lakefront residents sought new lots and/or abodes near the Washington Park addition to Indiana Harbor. The earlier immigrants and Native Americans joined them as well, leaving the Block and Pennsylvania avenues area to be settled by African American migrants and Mexican immigrants during World War I. African Americans also settled in the immigrant section of Hunkytown.

This residential pattern solidified in the ensuing decades, as the "Workshop of America" blossomed in the first half of the twentieth century. The growth and development of Inland Steel and the Twin City amazed observers. A new neighbor to the east, however, would both rival and complement the Twentieth Century Wonder.

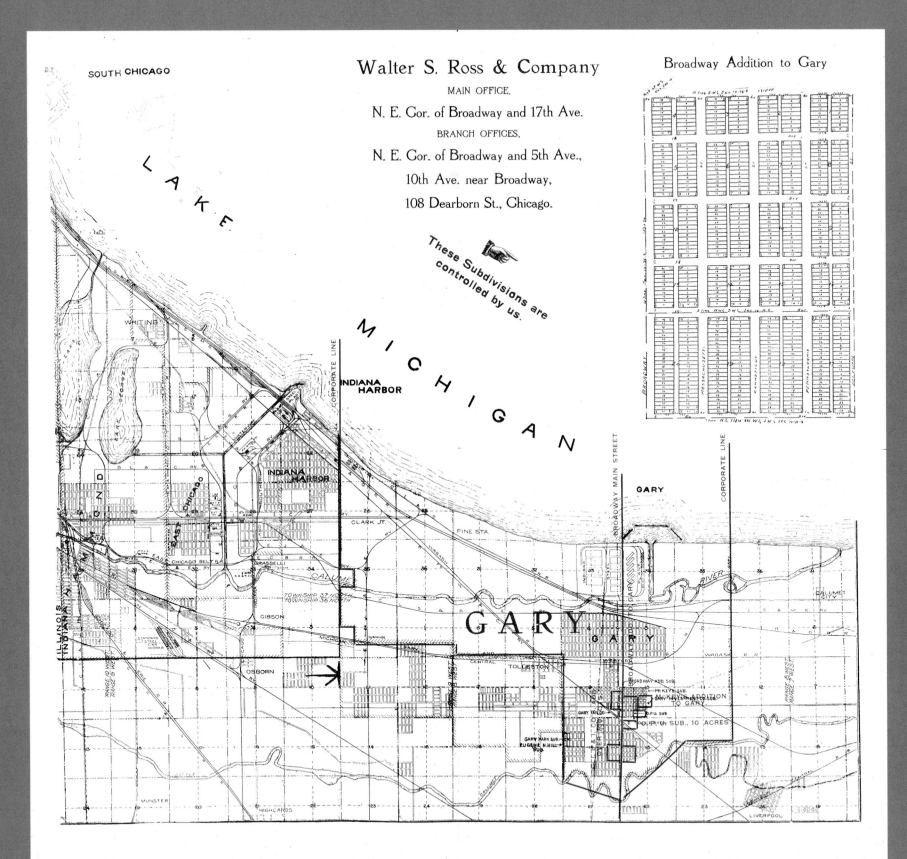

Figure Intro.4. Map of Northwest Indiana ca. 1910

Steel Giant No. 2: U.S. Steel's Gary Works

"It has been decided to construct and put into operation a new plant to be located on the south shore of Lake Michigan, in Calumet Township, Lake County, Indiana, and a large acreage of land has been purchased for that purpose. It is proposed to construct a plant of the most modern standards. . . ." With these words in 1905, Elbert H. Gary, Chairman of the Board, United States Steel Corporation—and formerly a judge in DuPage County, Illinois—initiated what contemporaries called "the industrial wonder of the world." U.S. Steel's Gary Works was, indeed, a monumental achievement. The construction of the world's largest integrated steel mill climaxed the dynamic post–Civil War growth of the nation's steel industry and symbolized the incredible power and might of American industrial development in the early twentieth century.

Despite its success during its first five years, U.S. Steel could not meet demand, particularly in the Midwest, and many of its mills were aging. Judge Gary realized a new, modern integrated mill complex was needed. After much discussion, the Corporation settled on a northwest Indiana site in the Calumet region and named it after Judge Gary. The site attracted the judge's interest for the same reasons that brought Standard Oil, Inland Steel, and other heavy industry to the region: plentiful, cheap land for industrial expansion; low taxes; a rail network comprising five major lines; abundant water supplies for production and transportation; and proximity to Midwest markets and the Chicago labor supply. The Gary site was, in short, the perfect place to build the world's largest integrated steel mill.

In contrast to the somewhat piecemeal, but steady, growth of Inland Steel's Indiana Harbor Works and the Indiana Harbor section of East Chicago, the Corporation carefully planned both its Gary Works and its portion of the city of Gary. In addition, whereas East Chicago lured a potpourri of industry into its tightly packed borders, U.S. Steel sought to maintain its hold on its steeltown by discouraging active recruitment of potential competitors. Instead, the Corporation pursued a strategy of subtle domination in its newest enterprise.

Once Judge Gary had decided on the Calumet region site in 1905, U.S. Steel Corporation wasted no time in acquiring the necessary land. Corporation attorney Armanis F. Knotts (a former mayor of Hammond) quietly began purchasing tracts, eventually totaling 9,000 acres along seven miles of Lake Michigan shoreline and nearly two miles south to the Wabash railroad tracks. The cost for this land approached $7.2 million dollars. U.S. Steel formed a subsidiary, the Indiana Steel Company, to construct Gary Works.

On March 12, 1906, construction engineers, led through a snowstorm by Chief Construction Engineer Ralph E. Rowley, began laying out the mill, harbor, and railroad yards. By early summer, teams of horses and mules (many from area farms) began leveling and grading the dunes on the lakeshore. Buildings and facilities rose rapidly above the sand and swamps, creating an impressive industrial skyline. The engineers relocated the Grand Calumet River, the "moat" between the southern end of the mill site and the north end of the town site, and also redirected three major rail lines traversing the area.

The Corporation had envisioned a massive mill complex, and it was not disappointed. Over twelve million cubic yards of sand were removed. Foundations for the mill structures required two million yards of concrete. The railroad yards could hold 15,000 cars. A mile-long harbor was built, 25 feet deep and 250 feet wide, between two parallel piers extending 2,360 feet into Lake Michigan; it included a turning basin 750 feet in diameter to accommodate the huge iron ore boats.

In just over two years, on July 23, 1908, the oreboat Elbert H. Gary entered Gary Works harbor with the first load of iron ore. In December, the first of twelve blast furnaces began producing iron. On February 3, 1909, two open hearths tapped the first heats of steel and the rail mill produced its first finished product. By the end of the year, 6,800 employees had produced 570,000 tons of steel.

Both steel production and mill construction continued at an accelerated pace. By 1920, Gary Works contained 12 blast furnaces, 838 coke ovens, 45 open hearth furnaces, 2 twenty-five-ton converters, a rail mill, a billet mill, a slabbing mill, 2 plate mills, 12 merchant mills, an axle mill, a tie plate mill, a steel wheel plant, and a dozen mechanical shops covering 300,000 square feet. The buildings embraced more than 100,000 tons of structural steel, 9,000 tons of corrugated sheets, 4,000 squares of tile roofing, and 163,000,000 bricks.

Consistent with Judge Gary's philosophy of integrated, efficient continuous production, the steelmaking process flowed from east to west: raw materials (primarily coal) were converted

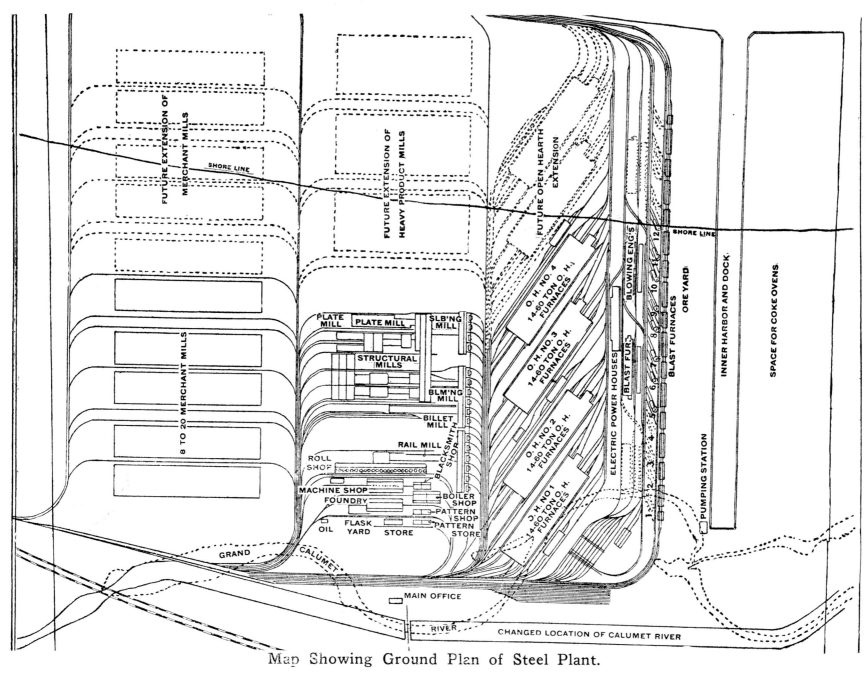

Map Showing Ground Plan of Steel Plant.

Figure Intro.5. Plant layout, U.S. Steel Gary Works

to coke in the coke ovens, and entered the blast furnaces, along with iron ore and limestone (from Minnesota and Michigan, via Lake Michigan), creating molten iron, which was poured into Bessemer converters and/or open hearth furnaces. The resulting steel was then poured into ingot molds for shaping into plates, rails, bars, and slabs, and eventually processed into finished products. Gary Works, along with other U.S. Steel subsidiaries located near the original mill, produced raw steel, rails, wire, hoops, tin plate, rods, pipes, tubes, sheets, wheels, axles, and cement. In rapid, efficient fashion, Gary Works became U.S. Steel's flagship plant and assumed the leadership role among steelmakers in the Calumet region and across the nation. Between 1906 and 1930, U.S. Steel's Gary Works truly became one of the industrial wonders of the twentieth century.

Gary, Indiana: City of the Century

In contrast to the Inland Steel Company's directors, U.S. Steel officials sought to construct a model company town for the skilled workers, foremen, and supervisors. The Corporation poured resources into the design and construction of Gary. U.S. Steel created a subsidiary, the Gary Land Company, to design the city. The Land Company's president, Eugene J. Buffington, noted the corporation's pragmatic view of the city plan: "Gary is nothing more than the product of effort along practical lines to secure the right living conditions around a steel manufacturing plant." The Gary Land Company succeeded in that mission, at least in its First Subdivision, extending south from the plant site to about 9th Avenue. Although the city grew beyond this border, the actual company-constructed town resided in the First Subdivision.

U.S. Steel's First Subdivision enjoyed paved streets, landscaped residential areas, a booming downtown district, and pleasant company housing. Planners deliberately avoided, however, the experiences of paternalistic company towns such as Pullman, Illinois, where the company had owned all housing and dictated the morals and social behavior of the workers. Instead, U.S. Steel desired a more subtle form of influence over town affairs, letting employees own their own homes while the company sold lots and provided mortgages. Although non-corporation businesses and homes flourished in the First Subdivision, the company dictated strict regulations on building and design.

Built simultaneously with the mill, the First Subdivision comprised 800 acres, platted into 4,000 lots; each block included 40 residential lots. Streets were designed in grid fashion, parallel to two major thoroughfares, 5th Avenue (east–west) and Broadway (north–south). Businesses along these main streets had to rise at least two stories and be built of stone or brick. The residential areas were well-manicured, with paved streets, sidewalks, young shade trees, and topsoil. Another U.S. Steel subsidiary, the Gary Heat, Light, and Water Company, provided free water for trees and lawns for four months a year. The Gary Land Company installed all utilities and sewers. U.S. Steel donated lots for parks, churches, a public library, a YMCA, and other buildings. The First Subdivision also included a booming downtown business district, with the hub at 5th and Broadway.

Employees could purchase lots from the Land Company but had to adhere to strict building regulations, including erecting a building within eighteen months. Only the very well-paid employees could meet this requirement, so the Gary Land Company began to build, sell, and/or rent houses for supervisors, foremen, and skilled workers. Five hundred and six houses in a variety of styles and price ranges were offered for sale or rent, depending on the income and status of the employee; most were rented at rates determined by the model and location in the First Subdivision.

By 1908, two years after mill and town began construction, the Corporation had spent $42,000,000 on the mill and town projects. Local boosters referred to Gary as the Magic City and the City of the Century.

Unfortunately, while the Corporation erected a modern state-of-the-art mill town in its north side First Subdivision, it virtually ignored the southern end of the city outside of its property. Living in the First Subdivision was out of reach for the bulk of the Gary Works workforce, most of whom were foreign-born laborers. Mirroring the mixing bowl of Indiana Harbor, by 1920, fifty-two nationalities made their home in Gary, along with a significant number of African American migrants from the south and Mexican workers from south of the border. The newcomers lived in the southern area of the city, known as the Patch. There a very different Gary evolved, with numerous shacks, saloons, and overcrowded boarding houses, along with a proliferation of real estate speculation and unsanitary conditions. A mining camp atmosphere prevailed, including more than 200 saloons, with names such as the Bucket of Blood. Gambling and prostitution flourished. Unpaved streets, no sewage facilities, and no running water were trademarks of the Patch.

As historian James B. Lane has described, the Gary police chief at the time referred to the Patch as "hell on wheels." For a time, the red-light district was cordoned off with barbed wire. Sidewalks, where there were any, were stained with blood. Another Gary historian, Richard Meister, offered this view:

> Here men drank, brawled, and sometimes died. Here charming streetwalkers sold their wares in a way any of the fifty-plus nationalities could understand. Here men either stashed away their wages in order to return to the homeland to a comfortable life or to bring their wife or mail-order bride over or gambled and drank away every sweated penny.

Eventually, the new immigrants would be able to improve their socioeconomic lot and move out of the Patch. As the city matured, the neighborhood received city services and most of the old saloons and shacks disappeared, replaced by comfortable homes, thriving businesses, restaurants, and clubs. The area became known as the Central District or Midtown and was a city within a city, as the African American population remained strictly segregated in the Central District until the color line was broken later in the twentieth century.

As with its industrial neighbor to the west, Gary grew dramatically in its first fifty years. The 1910 census revealed a population of 16,802; in 1920, 55,378; by 1930, 100,426. Twenty years later, 133,719 residents called Gary home. As Gary Works and the City of the Century celebrated their golden jubilee in 1956, times were good in the region's largest city. At that point, the population stood at 168,601 and U.S. Steel's Gary Works covered 2,700 acres, employed more than 20,000 workers, and enjoyed a steelmaking capacity of 7,204,000 tons of steel. Gary residents, along with their counterparts in East Chicago, believed there would be no stopping this fast and steady growth. The situation would change dramatically just twenty years later.

Capturing the Steel Giants on Film

The photographs compiled in this volume offer a visual journey through the brief history sketched in this introduction, documenting primarily the first fifty years of life of these steelmakers and their steel towns. During this period, Inland Steel and U.S. Steel founded their behemoths and expanded them so that by the 1950s, the stage was set for even greater growth and expansion, up to the precipitous decline later in the century. While not comprehensive, we have attempted to select images that depict the size of these two steel plants and capture the drama of steelmaking. While perusing these scenes, keep in mind that the selection of photographs was limited by the contents of the two visual collections created by Inland Steel and U.S. Steel housed in the Calumet Regional Archives. Additional images of these plants and cities exist in other collections and in other repositories and have been used in a variety of other publications and pictorial histories.

Our goal is to bring the reader back to a time of incredible industrial might which defined a region and its people. We hope you enjoy the trip.

Bolt and Nut Shop, ca. 1920.
Inland Steel Company Indiana
Harbor Works

The Story of an Inland Galvanized Sheet

By 1911, ten years after groundbreaking for its Indiana Harbor Works, the Inland Steel Company's sales force was armed with literature, such as this booklet, to sway potential customers into becoming steady users of Inland products. The booklet details the steelmaking process and stresses particularly the use of the open hearth and galvanizing methods to produce quality steel sheet. Customers unfamiliar with how steel was made found this booklet to be a very useful introduction, and we hope the reader will find it similarly helpful.

This is the Life-Story of an "Inland" Sheet.

In so small a book only a small part of the story can be told, and the hardest task confronting the writer of it is to decide what to leave unsaid—it is all so interesting.

It is also an unique story, for practically no other independent sheet steel industry in America has such absolute control of every step, from ore to finished product, as the "Inland" has.

It is a story of "Inland" Ore Mines, "Inland" Blast Furnaces, "Inland" Basic Open Hearth Furnaces, "Inland" Blooming-Mills, "Inland" Sheet Bar Mills, "Inland" Sheet-Rolling Mills, "Inland" Galvanizing Pots—not a step missing in the forward march of the product; not a weak link in the chain of modern appliances that are there for one purpose—the creation of the perfect galvanized sheet.

Furthermore, it is the story of the Basic Open Hearth Process in its highest state of modern development—a glimpse into a model plant, so highly perfected that it is visited by steel makers from every corner of the industrial world—from Russia in the East to Japan and China in the west.

The Story *of an*
Inland Galvanized Sheet

1911

Inland Steel Company

First National Bank Building

Chicago

Works: Indiana Harbor, Indiana

WHAT INLAND SHEETS ARE
Before exploring into the parentage and pedigree of Inland Sheets let us look at the sheets themselves and take the testimony of our own eyes.

What do we see?

Black Open Hearth Sheets—using the term in the broad sense to include one-pass cold rolled sheets; blue annealed sheets; pickled, deep stamping, electrical and other highly finished sheets, and even ordinary red tank plate.

But, most important of all:

Inland Galvanized Open Hearth Sheets—the highest type of galvanized sheets that the skill of man has thus far produced—a statement that you will appreciate more fully after you have read this story of the making of an Inland Galvanized Basic Open Hearth Sheet; but whose full meaning you will never grasp till you have *worked* Inland Sheets side by side with the make that you had heretofore considered the most nearly perfect the art had yet produced.

CLAIMS AND THE REASON WHY
As this story progresses we shall unfold briefly and logically the reasons for the following claims for the superiority of Inland Galvanized Sheets:

1. *That Inland Sheets are the most workable;* contain the toughest and most ductile steel—basic open hearth steel—of the highest type.

2. *That Inland Sheets are the most beautiful*—not only the surface beauty of the magic spangling or frosting, painted by unseen forces of Nature, but the beauty that is more than skin-deep—the beauty of quality through-and-through.

3. *That the Inland Galvanizing surpasses all others* in its approach to rust-proofness and peel-proofness; its great power to resist the attacks of moisture, acid, fumes and all other enemies of iron and steel.

4. *That Inland Sheets are more free from defects* and "hard spots"; more true to weight, gauge and size; more uniform in texture; more workmanlike in finish than any other sheets, iron or steel, domestic or foreign.

This is our "brief," gentlemen of the jury, and all the evidence is at hand awaiting your pleasure.

Tipple and Stock Pile at Laura Mine, Hibbing, Minn.

CHAPTER I
MINING THE IRON ORE

To begin with—the ore.

You have heard of the wonderful "Mesaba Country" in Northeastern Minnesota—the greatest iron-ore deposit thus far discovered in the world—a storehouse of wealth surpassing the richest gold mines, and so near to the surface that the cost of mining is lower than in any other district in America.

So near the surface is it that we might almost scrape off the soil and sand and gravel on top, and scoop up the ore like red clay from a brickyard; but more important to you, a user of Inland Galvanized Sheets, is the *quality* of this ore, and our independent ownership of millions of tons of it as yet unmined. For the Inland Steel Company *owns* the Laura mine, just outside of the town of Hibbing, Minnesota; and Laura ore is the ideal ore for making the pure basic pig iron from which basic Open Hearth Steel is made.

It is what is known as a "*strong*" ore, as contrasted with the weak ores of the South, for instance. It is a strong ore because it makes a strong iron, and it *is* strong because it is high in manganese and relatively free from phosphorus.

You will understand more clearly how important this is as the story progresses, and will appreciate how fortunate we are to have the best of basic iron ores as a foundation for the best of basic steel sheets.

The picture at the top of the page shows the stock pile at Laura mine. There are many thousands of tons of ore in that pile, the accumulation of the winter months awaiting the opening of navigation in the spring.

Two Unloading Bridges at Inland Works, Indiana Harbor, Ind.

Appliances for loading the cars are so perfect that a train, like the one on the previous page, containing forty cars, is loaded at a trifling cost. Then comes a run at high speed to West Superior, about sixty-five miles away, ending at the world-famous ore docks. Here a pull of a lever opens the hopper-gate of each car, and the whole train can be unloaded in a few minutes.

The ore is either run direct through the ore "pockets" into the hold of a waiting ore-steamer or is stored in the "pockets" of the ore dock, there to wait till the next steamer ties up at the dock. In either case the vessel is loaded wholly by gravity—five thousand tons of ore being loaded in thirty minutes by this method.

A three-days' voyage brings the ore to our Indiana Harbor ore-docks, where the vessel is unloaded by means of grab-buckets that are lowered from the unloading "bridges" through the hatchways into the holds of the ships. Instantly each one of these buckets grabs about seven tons of ore at a mouthful and is whirled vertically by cables to the bridge above. Here the "grabs" are sent spinning to the other end of the bridge, where they deposit their load onto the stock pile beneath or direct into the bins of the blast furnace.

Ten thousand tons of ore can be unloaded in a single working day at the company's ore docks at Indiana Harbor.

As navigation is closed during the winter months the company provides storage capacity for 300,000 tons of ore.

That would make a train of loaded ore cars fifty miles long!

These unloading machines—there are two of them—are of the latest type. When you realize that the great steel steamer shown in the cut is over a city block long you get an idea of the magnitude of the ore-unloading equipment at Inland Works.

The Madeline Blast Furnace, Part of Inland Works at Indiana Harbor

CHAPTER II

SMELTING THE ORE

Iron ore is a mixture of iron oxide and earthy matter. To separate the iron from its earthy entanglement it is necessary to smelt the whole mass so that in its liquid form the heavier iron sinks to the bottom and the lighter mineral-slag which contains the impurities floats on top of the molten iron and is skimmed off.

It requires a heat of almost inconceivable fury to smelt iron ore—no less than 3000° F.

This heat is secured from the combustion of the finest grade of Connellsville coke by means of a fierce blast of hot air that is forced through it—hence the name Blast Furnace.

A blast furnace is a huge retort or crucible built from highly refractory fire brick, inside a heavy steel plate jacket.

The Inland Blast Furnace—the Madeline—is of the most modern construction, 85 feet high.

Every fifteen to twenty minutes, night and day, a charge is made by means of the two steel "skip cars"—one loaded with ore and another with limestone or coke, which run up the inclined railroad to the top of the blast furnace, and automatically dump their loads into the top of the stack.

In the olden days men, inured to incredible heat, had to dump these charges into the furnace top; but nowadays mechanical devices step in to relieve man of undue exposure in every step in the steel industry.

A charge is made by the skip-cars in this wise:

First, a charge of the most expensive Connellsville coke is dumped in—almost pure carbon, free from sulphur.

Then several tons of ore; then a charge of limestone—in all 1800 tons a day, going into the hungry mouth of the furnace.

The limestone is put in to act as a "flux;" that is, to make the ore melt and flow more quickly. It also forms a chemical union with the minerals in the ore and makes them separate themselves more completely from the iron, and flow off in the slag or escape in the gases.

While this charging is being done at the top of the 85-foot furnace, the mass at the bottom is being drawn off at intervals of four hours. So the successive charges of the blast furnace sink down to make room for more at the top.

But how about the blast of hot air that helps do this work?

Notice the four tall cylindrical "tanks" in the picture on the opposite page. These are called "stoves." They are built of heavy plates of steel with a checker-work of fire brick filling nearly the whole interior.

Waste gas—highly inflammable—from the top of the blast furnace is carried into the first of these stoves and burned with so strong a draft of air produced by great stacks or chimneys 200 feet high that the fire brick becomes white hot. Then the gas is switched into the next stove and cold air is forced into the white-hot one. This cold air while being forced through the white-hot fire brick checker-work by powerful blowing engines is heated to from 1000 to 1300° F. before being driven into the hearth of the blast furnace, where it assists in reducing the ore. In this way each stove in its turn is made to supply its quota of superheated air to the blast furnace; and by the time No. 4 has done its work No. 1 is ready for its air-heating job.

The molten iron, freed from the slag that floats on it, is tapped into huge brick-lined ladles, each ladle holding about twenty tons. Each ladle sits on its own little car, and a whole trainload is filled at one cast.

This red-hot train pulled by an Inland locomotive hustles off through a tunnel to the open hearth furnaces, where the molten iron is poured direct into the Open Hearth Furnaces. In these furnaces it will be transformed into Basic Open Hearth Steel, as we shall see.

As the Open Hearth Furnaces do not run on Sundays and holidays a pig-iron casting machine is provided to take care of this surplus iron.

Trainloads of Molten Iron are Whizzed through a Tunnel from the Blast Furnace to the Steel Works Proper

Pouring the Molten Iron from the Blast Furnace into the Ladles that go Either Direct to the Open Hearth Furnaces or to the Pig Casting Machine

The Blast Furnace produces a daily average of between 400 and 500 tons of iron, most of which is carried direct into the Open Hearth Furnace as previously described, the pig-casting machines being only an incidental convenience to permit the uninterrupted forcing of the blast furnace.

UTILIZING THE WASTE GASES

The gas that is generated by burning the coke and smelting the ore is a splendid fuel gas.

And it is put to splendid use at the Inland Works. Part of it goes to the "stoves" previously described. The balance, hot from the top of the blast furnace tops, is carried direct to eight 500-horsepower boilers at the electrical powerhouse. The 4000 horsepower developed is used in running the hundreds of motors that operate ore unloading machines, the electric railway system, a hundred or so electric cranes, and, in fact, all the electrical machinery about the whole plant, including the electric-lighting systems.

Only a few years ago, even in America, all these priceless gases were permitted to escape in the air—a poison in place of a benefit; and many plants in England and on the Continent still use this wasteful method. But nothing is wasted at the Inland Works, not even words.

NORTHERN BASIC IRON

Ask any steel man what he thinks about the best Northern iron, and what kind of sheet steel he thinks it would make by the Basic process.

Then ask him what kind of steel would come from high-phosphorus Southern iron by either the acid open hearth or the acid Bessemer process—the processes, you know, that can't rid the steel of the phosphorus in the iron, but carry it over bodily.

Then when you get his answer you will appreciate what it means to the Inland Works to produce, as it does, only high-grade Northern Basic Iron, and to use only the Basic Open Hearth Process in turning that iron to steel.

The pig iron from the Madeline Blast Furnace analyzes as follows:

Silicon	1.00 per cent
Phosphorus	.14 " "
Manganese	1.35 " "
Sulphur	.03 " "

To the trained steel man this tells an eloquent story:

Low Silicon, to meet the requirements of the basic process.

Low Phosphorus—a tribute to the purity of the Laura ore and a lightening of the labor of the Open Hearth Steel men who will have to get rid of this small remainder.

High Manganese—one of the most valuable alloys that has ever been discovered—a toughener of steel, prized by makers of rails and armor plate for this reason. It is also valuable as an eliminator of impurities in the molten steel.

Low Sulphur—in fact almost none at all; and even this will be dissipated and carried away by the Basic Open Hearth Process of making steel from this iron, as you shall see.

The Pig Iron Casting Machine at Inland Works

Though most of our iron goes direct from the blast furnace to the open hearth furnaces, in ladles, without cooling, as described before, we make some pig iron.

You know the old way of making pig iron—running it out of the furnace-mouth into a series of long canals in a sand bed, and from those canals into little laterals, where it cooled into pigs. They call the canals "sows" and the little laterals "pigs;" hence the name pig iron.

But that was a slow and wasteful way, a lot of impurities often attached themselves to the iron, especially silica, the pigs were irregular in size and shape, and the expense of breaking up and remelting the sows was very considerable.

So somebody invented the pig-casting machine.

It is simply a long endless belt with steel buckets on it, each bucket being a mold for a 100-pound pig of iron.

The ladle car is brought into the casting house, the ladle poured by electricity, and the molten iron runs through a trough into the moving bucket conveyor.

By the time a bucket has reached the farther end of a slow journey to the top of the 200-foot incline you would think the iron would be hardened into pigs; but so great is the initial heat of the fluid iron that it is necessary to drench the molds in a flood of cold water on their upward journey.

Even then the pigs, when they drop out of the buckets at the upper end, are so hot that the car into which the machine drops them must be flooded with water to keep it from catching on fire.

The pig iron thus made is dumped onto a stock pile ready for charging into the Open Hearth Furnaces when needed.

A Row of Open Hearth Furnaces in Inland Works

CHAPTER III

SUPERIORITY OF BASIC OPEN HEARTH STEEL

Steel is made from iron by several different processes.

Nowadays, the three leading kinds are Bessemer Steel, Acid Open Hearth Steel and Basic Open Hearth Steel.

Bessemer Steel is made by blowing air through a "converter" full of molten iron until all the carbon is burned out of it; then adding whatever percentage of carbon is desired. This process leaves in the steel practically all the phosphorus and sulphur that were in the ore, making the steel relatively hard and brittle.

Acid Open Hearth is also inferior in its results, being nothing more than a remelting process, as all the sulphur and phosphorus in the pig iron are carried over into the steel, the carbon and silicon only being eliminated. The term "acid" means simply that the furnace has a silicate lining, made from ordinary silica sand, and silicon is an acid. It is used because it makes a cheap brick that will withstand the heat required for melting iron. Silicon is an enemy to a good steel sheet, because it makes steel hard and brittle.

Basic Open Hearth is named from the fact that the open hearth furnace is given a basic lining. A basic mineral is one that is wholly free from silicon or other acid. It is not only not acid but is actually alkaline. The basic lining used for Open Hearth furnaces is Magnesite, a claylike substance imported from Austria. It is put into the furnaces so that lime may be added to the melt, something that cannot be done when an acid lining is used, for the lime at once attacks the acid lining and destroys it.

Lime is put into the molten charge so that the alkali of the lime will unite with the undesirable sulphur and phosphorus in the iron and carry them off in the slag and in the escaping gases. Sulphur makes steel rotten when hot, and brittle when cold, and phosphorus makes it both brittle and rotten when cold.

The Basic Open Hearth Process makes a steel free from these enemies—a steel that is practically pure iron, except for the necessary percentage of carbon. Chemically pure iron without carbon, something obtainable only in a laboratory, is almost as soft as lead, can easily be cut with a knife, and is, of course, useless as a commercial commodity.

Steel must have about one-tenth of one per cent carbon to be strong and tough. Too much carbon makes it brittle.

The Basic Open Hearth Process makes it possible to regulate the carbon in iron to the exact fraction desired; and one of the great elements of the popularity of the Inland Steel Company is its ability and its willingness to supply any analyses desired by purchasers of special steel for special purposes.

THE USE OF FUEL OIL

On top of the many advantages of the Inland equipment and processes previously described is the use of fuel oil instead of producer gas or natural gas in the various melting, heating and annealing processes that lead up to the finished Open Hearth Sheet.

Fuel oil costs more than any other fuel available for this purpose; but it is a better fuel, making a better steel, and that is why we use it. It makes a better steel because its flame is a *clean* flame, free from sulphur, while other fuels, and particularly producer gas, are foul with sulphur and other impurities. Not only does the use of fuel oil avoid the sulphur evil, but it also avoids a lot of trouble with scale and other surface blemishes that a "dirty" flame leaves in its wake.

Producer gas is gas made from coal by a number of different processes; but no means have yet been perfected for keeping out of the gas the sulphur that is in the coal. This is the grave problem that now confronts the steel industries in the Pittsburgh and the Ohio districts—the increasing percentage of sulphur in even the best available coals.

For a while natural gas partially solved this problem, but that supply is now practically exhausted.

Inland Works is fortunate in being next door neighbor to Whiting, Indiana—a city of oil tanks, home of the Standard Oil Company's largest refinery.

An "oil main" three miles long conveys fuel oil from Whiting to a 50,000-gallon storage tank in the Inland Works. From this tank it is pumped through a network of pipes to the thousands of jets that heat the open hearth furnaces, the annealing pits, sheet mill furnaces and other heating operations throughout the plant.

The Pouring Side of Open Hearth Furnaces in Inland Works

CHAPTER IV

THE OPEN HEARTH PROCESS ITSELF

Let us walk through that great 900-feet Open Hearth Building, with its eight sixty-ton furnaces.

A sixty ton furnace means a furnace that will produce sixty tons to a heat, and our habit of securing three such heats every twenty-four hours from each furnace that is in commission is considered "good practice" by expert steel makers the world over.

On one side of this battery of furnaces is the charging floor, somewhat elevated. A huge overhead charging machine travels the length of it and waits on the furnaces as a nurse does upon a row of beds in the ward of a hospital.

Let us watch a furnace—No. 7, the Bulletin Board says:

Though it is still hot from the last charge, men get as near to it as they can, and with proper tools plaster up, with magnesite and dolomite—two basic clays—the holes eaten in the basic lining by the last charge. Then a quantity of limestone is spread on the floor of the furnace, so that the burning of this lime will make the steel boil and throw off, in a gaseous form, the sulphur and phosphorus—two enemies that steel men hate worse than the devil is supposed to hate holy water.

Then high-grade scrap and other materials are charged by the same machine.

Last of all come ladles carrying a spitting, seething mass of white-hot iron, fresh from the blast furnace. The lower door of the furnace is closed and this molten mass is poured in through an upper door provided for the purpose.

At this instant the fuel oil burners are opened, and alongside of them jets of superheated steam under high pressure, and before you know it the iron that lies on the bed of the hearth, below this fiery blast, is boiling like water.

Now here is what happens inside of this furiously hot (4000° F.) Open Hearth furnace:

The carbon in the iron is burned out of it by the oxygen of the hot air, acting with the oxygen of the iron ore that is added to the melt.

The .14 of one per cent of phosphorus unites with the lime and forms a slag that is so rich in phosphorus that there is a ready demand for it as a commercial fertilizer, and another element of the lime and of the basic lining takes hold of the .03 of one per cent sulphur and drags it out of the iron, largely in the form of a gas, but partly in sulphate of magnesium, which you will perhaps recognize better under its drug-store name of epsom salts.

As steel must have carbon in it (just enough, and not a shade more or less for the purpose desired) the chemist in charge prescribes for each furnace exactly the right amount of carbon, and this is added to the melt after the excess has been eliminated.

This chemist, too, keeps sampling the melt as it proceeds in order to be sure that sulphur, phosphorus and all other bad elements are driven out of it, along with the carbon, and not until everything is exactly right will he permit a melt to be poured.

TESTING CHEMICALLY AS WELL AS BY FRACTURE

Another exclusive Inland feature. As far as we know, the Inland is the only mill in existence in which a chemical laboratory is operated on the floor of the Open Hearth department; the only one in which the melting steel is regularly tested *chemically* for impurities.

The regular practice in all mills—even in those most recently built in the West— is to test only by "fracture," that is, by cooling and breaking a test-sample drawn from the molten steel, and looking at the color and granulation of this fracture.

The "fracture-test" is a relic of the old rule-of-thumb days, liable to error; the chemical test is the *new* method of the *new era*, in which guesswork is replaced by scientific certainty.

And, by the way, the Inland chemist makes the fracture test, too, thus making doubly certain, by both chemical and physical tests, that the steel is both chemically and physically perfect before he permits it to be poured.

The chemist in the Open Hearth mill is the czar of the furnaces. When he says a furnace shall be tapped, it is tapped, and not till then; and he does not give the word till his chemical tests prove that every vestige of impurity has been driven out of the molten mass.

Views in Our Main Laboratory—Branch Laboratories are on the Open Hearth Floor

LABORATORIES

The splendidly equipped chemical and physical laboratories of the Inland Steel Company are maintained for our customers' protection as well as our own.

All ores are analyzed and ores of varying properties are combined in each blast so as to produce the best iron.

Test pieces of the iron of each melt are analyzed chemically and tested on special machines for tensile strength, elastic limit, etc. This is done in a sub-laboratory on the floor of the Open Hearth Department and the Inland is the only mill thus supplying the positive test of chemical analysis, plus the physical "fracture" test, to determine the purity of the steel before permitting the charge to be poured. In the steel-making process all the limestone, carbon, manganese and iron oxide added to the melt are determined by careful analysis, and during the melt test specimens are dipped out, cooled and analyzed and such ingredients are added as will be necessary to eliminate impurities or bring the steel to the exact analysis desired.

TAKE NO CHANCES

So strict are our orders, so rigid our rules of inspection, so positive our method of tracing responsibility for any oversight or error, that our chemists, our inspectors and all men whose judgment is relied upon to produce "Inland Quality," have learned that it pays to play safe, and that it is a whole lot better to be sure than sorry.

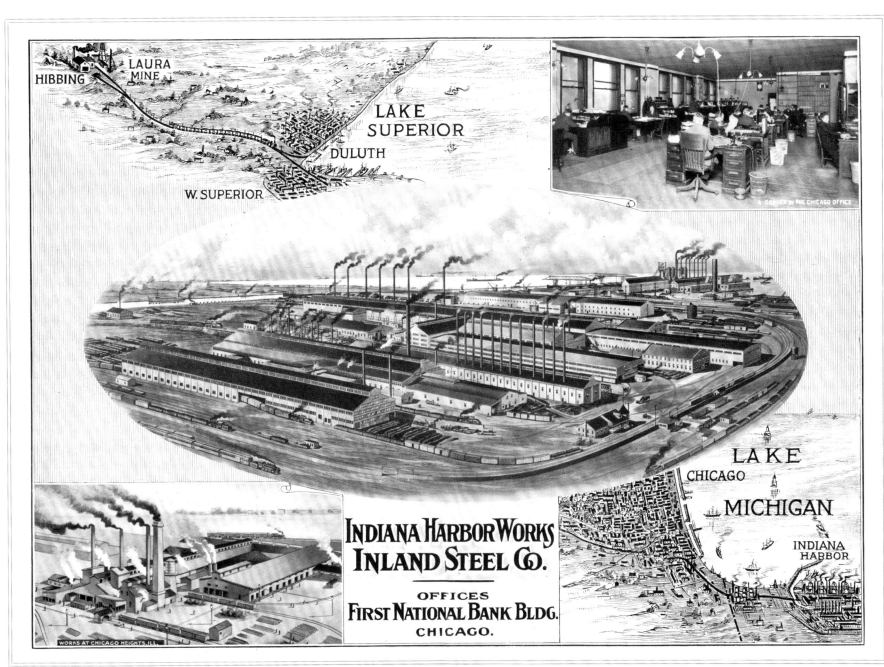

HIBBING

LAURA
MINE

LAKE
SUPERIOR

DULUTH

W. SUPERIOR

A CORNER IN THE CHICAGO OFFICE

LAKE

CHICAGO

MICHIGAN

INDIANA
HARBOR

INDIANA HARBOR WORKS
INLAND STEEL CO.

OFFICES
FIRST NATIONAL BANK BLDG.
CHICAGO.

WORKS AT CHICAGO HEIGHTS, ILL.

Pouring the Ingots—each Ingot Weighing 6500 Pounds

CHAPTER V
THE OPEN HEARTH INGOT

When this Open Hearth Steel is done to a turn—all the bad elements cooked out of it and all the good elements cooked *in*—it is drawn off at the rear into a huge ladle suspended from the 100-ton overhead traveling crane.

When the furnace is emptied the pouring orifice is closed and the ladle moves along to a row of ingot molds.

These ingot molds are tall squarish cast iron boxes, set in twos on heavy cast iron bases called stools. A two-inch trap at the bottom of the ladle is opened, and one after another of these ingot-molds is filled with the molten steel—each holding 6500 pounds.

The molds are filled as they stand on waiting cars, and the train of spitting, boiling, smoking, red-hot molds is pulled out into the yard, where, after they have sufficiently cooled and hardened, they are run under the "stripper."

This is an ingenious and extremely powerful machine that pulls the mold off the ingot. Enormous steel grippers, looking like the claws of a giant lobster, descend and grip the mold near the top, lifting it bodily from the car. Then a steel ram descends and pushes the ingot out through the bottom of the mold, leaving it standing on end—still red-hot—on the car, passing on to the next mold, till the whole row stands stripped and glowing.

These glowing ingots look to be ready for rolling, but they are not; for their heat is unevenly distributed—making them hard on the outside and almost molten in the center.

So the train of stripped red-hot ingots proceeds on its journey into the rolling-mill.

At one side of this huge building a row of twelve pits, "Soaking Pits" they are called, is sunk into the ground. These pits are made of fire brick, and a blast of coal gas flame from all sides makes them a veritable inferno.

Ingot Stripper

At a signal from the pit-boss a lever is turned and the ponderous brick-and-steel cover of a pit is slid off by hydraulic power. Meanwhile the overhead crane has swung down a grappling hook and seized a fiery ingot from

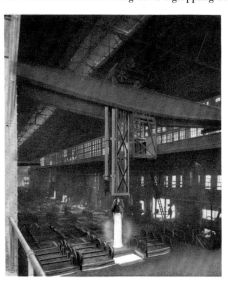

its car, bearing it swaying through the air, steadying it, for an instant, above the open pit, then lowering it to the depths of white-hot hell below. With the precision of a pendulum the cover is rolled back, the crane returns for another ingot, and the operation is repeated till each of the twelve pits has its full load of eight ingots "in soak."

The temperature of these soaking pits is just enough to bring the ingots to a white heat, and not enough to melt them. When the steel is at exactly the right heat it is lifted out and swung over onto the table of the blooming-mill.

Lowering an Ingot into one of the "Soaking Pits"

"A Crash like a Cannon Shot—an Instant of Struggle for Supremacy"

THE BLOOMING-MILL

A Blooming-mill is suggestive of anything rather than the blossoming of flowers. It is a big, ugly, noisy machine for fighting hot steel into submission.

In the center are huge steel rolls revolved toward each other by an 8000 h.p. engine. Leading to this is a long train of smaller rollers—table rolls—driven at a rapid rate; and the instant an ingot is laid on the far end of the table it begins its fiery journey to the jaws of the grooved rolls. When it strikes them there is a crash like a cannon shot—an instant of struggle for supremacy, but only an instant, for the ingot surrenders and is forced through the rolls, emerging not 21 inches thick as it was before, but about 19 inches, and considerably greater in length.

Back again it goes through a smaller groove in the same rolls, then forward another "pass" and so on through seventeen passes till it is reduced to a long flat slab $7\frac{1}{2}$x$3\frac{1}{2}$ inches in section.

THE CROPPING SHEAR

As this slab leaves the blooming-mill both the top and bottom ends are cut off by a huge shear known as the cropping shear, and these cropped ends are sent to the scrap heap. This cropping is done in order to make sure that the slab is free from seams, "pipes," blowholes and other defects and impurities that are often found at the top and bottom of ingots. So fine is our steel that we are offered fancy prices for these crop ends by other steel mills that want to use our low-phosphorus, low-sulphur "scrap" (practically only a trace of either) to reduce the too-high percentage of these enemies in their own product.

In reducing the ingot to a slab, and a slab to a sheet bar, it requires a judgment and skill little short of absolute genius to keep the metal at its best.

For steel is a fickle thing. It dare not be punished too severely; it must be nursed, coddled, coaxed, wheedled; but with a firmness that brooks no rebellion.

"A Long, Snakelike Strip of Steel"

The men who attend to this work regulate the successive "passes" wholly by the elongation of the bar being rolled, and they know instinctively just how much elongation the given thickness at a given heat will produce the best results. Uniform elongation is the key to good steel-making, and that is a trick that our men have mastered to a marked degree.

ROLLING THE SHEET BAR

From the blooming-mill the $7\frac{1}{2}$x$3\frac{1}{2}$-inch slabs pass automatically and continuously to the table of the sheet bar mill. The same operation as we saw in the blooming-mill is here repeated, though on a smaller scale, and the resulting sheet bar is a long, snakelike strip of steel varying in thickness according to the length and gauge of sheet that is to be rolled from it.

This red-hot sheet bar travels onward, after its last pass through the rolls to a saw, which cuts it into 30-feet lengths. A shrill crash, a shower of sparks, and the saw has severed a piece of steel thick enough to support a locomotive.

These 30-feet sheet bars are then assembled in piles weighing 10,000 pounds to the pile, and lifted to the cooling beds by the crane. After they have remained on the cooling beds until they are nearly cool they are transferred by another crane to the stock yard of the sheet mill, and every pile is marked with a serial number, indicating its heat-number and various specifications about the history of its rolling.

In the early days of our galvanized sheet-steel making we lacked one thing—a dependable supply of sheet bars.

Our blast furnace was not yet built and our Open Hearth furnaces were not sufficient to supply nearly the tonnage necessary. So we were forced to buy sheet bars from other mills, just as practically all the "independent" sheet mills buy them today. Those were days full of trouble, as we have described elsewhere.

General View of Sheet-rolling Mill

**Two Views in Inland Sheet Steel Mill
The Largest and Best Equipped Independent Sheet Steel Plant in the United States**

First Rolling or Roughing Out of the Sheet

CHAPTER VI

ROLLING THE SHEETS

The sheet rolling mill is a building 1300 feet long and 100 feet wide. Through the center of it runs a row of eighteen sheet mills of different sizes and widths. Ranged beside these in a parallel row is a series of furnaces.

The sheared sheet-bars previously described are brought into the building from the adjoining stock pile, after having been taken to a shear on which they were cut to whatever lengths were necessary to make the sheets of the width required by the rolling-mills.

These cut sheet bars are charged into an oil-burning pair heating furnace where they are brought up to a temperature of 1100 to 1400 degrees Fahrenheit. In the process of bringing these bars up to the required heat great care has to be exercised to prevent scale from forming on the bars.

When the bars attain a soft heat they are taken to the roughing rolls, where they are given one, two or three passes between the rolls according to the thickness of the bar, the bar being swept with a wire broom between every pass to free it from all scale, dirt and oxide.

Upon leaving the roughing rolls, the bars, reduced in thickness but otherwise larger, are taken to the hot finishing mill, where they are again reduced, to about one-third of their original thickness. This operation is called moleing down or roughing out. After the above operation the sheets are matched or piled in packs of three or four sheets. The packs are then put into oil-burning sheet furnaces where they are brought up to a temperature of between 900 to 1100 degrees Fahrenheit. The packs are then drawn from the sheet furnace and given one or two passes through the rolls. This causes them to adhere slightly. They are then opened up and doubled over, the packs of three sheets making six, and the packs of four sheets making eight sheets. This operation is called running over.

The packs or sheets are now ready for the final heat treatment and finish After the doubling over of the sheets they are returned to the sheet furnace, where they are again brought to a temperature of from 900 to 1100 degrees Fahrenheit. They are then drawn from the furnace one pack at a time and finished by the roller, he passing them between the rolls using the screws after each pass to give the proper draft upon his next pass until he has reduced this pack to the specified gauge and length.

This operation is called finishing. It requires great skill and long experience upon the part of the roller and heater, and any lack of judgment or want of skill on the part of these two men means absolute loss of the material being rolled.

Trimming and Squaring Shears

TRIMMING AND SQUARING

Under the eyes of the keen inspector the sheets are then lifted by power onto the table of the sheet shears—huge electrical guillotines—and the 12-foot knives descend and clip off the steel edges as easily as if they were paper to the exact dimensions specified in the order.

One Row of Cold-rolling Mills, Inland Works. See page opposite

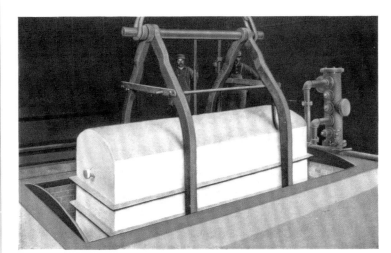

Lowering the Annealing Box full of Sheets into Annealing Oven

COLD ROLLING

You are familiar with the phrase, "One-pass, cold rolled sheet steel." That means simply that the sheets, after being hot rolled, are given a final rolling when cold. The cold rolls do not differ greatly from the hot rolls in general appearance, and the principle of their operation is the same. While the pressure exerted on these rolls is so great that it actually flattens the cold sheet of steel a shade thinner, the purpose of cold rolling is to take out the "waves" that hot rolling leaves in a sheet, and to clean up the surface so that it is bright and perfect. This last squeeze also adds to the toughness and density of the sheet, just as a blacksmith hammers tensile strength into a piece of iron.

Cold rolling is also an inspecting process, for any sheet with a flaw or defect that escaped all the many inspections that preceded is at once thrown out.

ANNEALING

The sheets are put together in "packs" and loaded into a huge portable furnace or box built of iron and fire brick. This box itself weighs several tons and it holds about fifteen tons of sheets; but when filled and sealed it is lifted jauntily by a crane and lowered into an oil-heated pit, there to remain, under an even cherry-red heat, for twelve hours, cooling gradually thereafter for twenty-four hours.

The fundamental principle of annealing is to hold the steel at an even heat—exactly the right heat—in what is practically a vacuum, because it is important that not a trace of oxygen from air, or from any other source, reaches the sheets during this operation. For this reason the annealing boxes are air-tight and

Pickling the Sheets

hermetically sealed, and the annealing pits also have covers that are sealed on tight. It is important, too, that no sulphur should be present during annealing, and here, too, lies the advantage that the Inland enjoys over other mills, as our annealing is done wholly with fuel oil—a fuel that is absolutely free from sulphur.

When the annealing is finished the box is raised out of its pit, allowed to cool in another sealed pit (away from the oxygen of the air), and when cool is opened, the sheets lifted out by a crane and swung on a trolley to the next operation.

In the care and scientific skill with which this annealing is done lies the greatest secret of the workability of the Inland Sheet, and no operation in our whole plant is carried on with greater care than this.

PICKLING

After the annealing comes the pickling. This is done in great vats filled with a sulphuric acid solution that eats off cinder, scale and any other foreign substance that may still lodge on the sheets, without appreciably attacking the metal itself. Sheets in packs are lowered edgewise into this vat, and a huge agitator that rises and falls at intervals forces a flood of the acid up and down between the sheets until they are as bright as a new dollar.

These shining sheets, smoking from their hot bath, are next given a drenching of cold "Lake Michigan," a great volume of clear cold water washing from their sides every vestige of the sulphuric acid from the pickling bath.

The sheets are completely submerged in vats of water until the galvanizing department is ready to run the sheets through the fluxing bath. This treatment prevents any oxide forming on the sheets. When any oxide, dirt or foreign matter is on the sheets the spelter will not adhere, and in forming or fabricating such sheets into various shapes the spelter will crack and peel off.

Galvanizing Pots

CHAPTER VII
GALVANIZING

The purpose of this pamphlet is to tell how an Inland Galvanized Sheet is made. We have shown briefly the making of the sheet itself, though we have had to omit scores of points, important in themselves, but too technical to come within the range of this booklet.

Suffice it to say that the naked, shining, open hearth sheets, when they enter the spelter pot, are the best, the toughest, the softest, and the most uniformly excellent steel that the genius of man has developed up to date; costing us more per ton, as far as we are able to learn, than any other sheet mill expends on its product.

And all this beautiful steel is to be covered up with a "silver" coat of spelter.

How easy it would be for us to "whitewash" *inferior* sheets with this spelter coat, if we were looking for *present* profits only.

And we could do this in a way that would leave ninety-nine out of a hundred customers none the wiser. Doing it, we could quickly earn the reputation of being the *cheapest* house in the business, cutting prices, yet making large profits.

But that is not the Inland way. If it were we would not urge our customers, and permit our competitors, to visit our plant, and stay as long as they wanted.

There are no secrets and no locked doors at Inland Works.

Before the sheets enter the galvanizing pot they are passed through a bath containing a special acid that makes doubly sure the sheets are perfectly clean and ready for the fluxing bath, on the same principle that your tinner washes the surface of the metal to be soldered before he applies the solder. This fluxing bath prepares the surface of the sheet so that the spelter will adhere to it for all time.

The spelter pot isn't a pot at all; does not even faintly suggest a pot. Rather is it a deep, square, steel vat filled with molten spelter. Spelter is zinc, and we'll have something to tell you about that, too, a little further on.

We told about the fluxing bath. This is at the front of the spelter pot, and the sheet is fed by guides through this bath and over into the spelter bath. In the bottom of this great pot of molten spelter is also a pair of rolls that continue to propel the sheet along its way through the bottom of the molten metal, while curved metal guides feed it onward and upward through the metal and through another pair of rolls at the farther edge of the pot. This last pair of rollers deflects the sheet upward against a curved guide, where for an intsant it stands flapping in the air, then falls gently downward onto a belt conveyor that carries it some 80 feet through a cleft in the wall into the next section of the building.

As the sheet emerges from the hot spelter it presents a plain silvery surface; but the instant the cooling begins, Nature, the greatest of all artists, begins painting the feathery "spangles" on its surface. This is a form of crystallization of the spelter exactly on the same principle as the crystallization of moisture in the form of frost on a window pane in cold weather.

And the patterns of the two are very much alike.

This spangling of the sheet is the secret of the selling-quality of the sheet, for men will judge sheets of steel by their outward appearances just as men judge each other.

Men make mistakes, too, in judging sheets, just as they do in judging each other; for the most showy is not always the most worthy. Ask any sheet buyer to take his choice between a sheet with large, showy, highly artistic spangles, and one with very small ones, and he will choose the showy sheet.

He may be wrong, or he may be right—depending on circumstances. Big spangles mean that the sheet cooled quickly. This quick cooling may mean a thin coat of spelter or it may mean that the sheet was galvanized in cold weather. Conversely, small spangles mean either an extra thick coat of spelter or an extra warm day at the mill when the sheet was coated.

We care little about the *size* of the "pictures" that Nature paints on our sheets; what we aim to do is to *make these pictures stick tighter* than others make them; in other words, to put on our galvanizing so that it *will not peel*, and so that it will keep moisture and fumes and acids and gases and all other enemies away from the steel of the sheet the longest possible time.

We do several things to insure this permanency to our galvanizing. In the first place we buy only prime virgin spelter, paying more for it than the market price for ordinary grades.

In the next place we prepare our sheets more carefully than most mills think necessary, giving them a surface so uniformly clean that there will be no spots to which the spelter will fail to fix itself firmly.

As spelter is *almost* a precious metal, and we buy thousands of tons of it, you can well imagine that the extra-heavy coating we give them costs us a pretty sum every year.

Every Sheet is Inspected on Both Sides

INSPECTION

The spirit of the Inland Works is the spirit of striving to excel. Every step in every process through which the product passes is accompanied by a most rigid inspection.

The expression "good enough" is never used. Unless the product can leave each process in practically a *perfect* condition, it is not permitted to leave at all. So true is this that the motto of every Inland inspector is

> "When in Doubt
> **REJECT**"

The picture at the top of this page shows, by photograph, one of the most rigid of all our many inspections.

At the end of each conveyor that carries the sheet from the galvanizing pot stands a trained expert who lifts each sheet singly from its conveyor, carefully scans both sides for the slightest defect, and, when he's in doubt, he *rejects* and sends the offending sheet back for regalvanizing.

To the untrained eye the pile of rejects on his "go-back" truck looks just about as fine as the sheets he passes on to the shipping room or warehouse.

Shipping Floor on Side of Warehouse—Room for a train of Thirty Cars

STORAGE WAREHOUSE AND WHAT IT MEANS

"Oh, I can't buy my galvanized sheets direct from a mill; it takes too long," say hundreds of sheet buyers nowadays.

To overcome this well-taken objection we have completed a sheet warehouse 1183 feet long, capable of storing thousands of tons of sheets.

And in this warehouse we are striving to accumulate so great a stock of all commercial sizes in each of the standard gauges that we shall be able to fill any order for straight carloads, or mixed carloads, from stock at mill in a few hours.

SHIPPING FACILITIES

Along one side of this warehouse is a great switch track and loading platform at which thirty cars may be loaded at once.

Our system for handling orders is on a par with our great manufacturing, warehousing and shipping facilities, and *"accuracy with dispatch"* is the guiding principle of this department.

Corrugating Machine at Work

CHAPTER VIII

INLAND GALVANIZED ROOFING AND SIDING

Soon after we entered the market as makers of galvanized sheets, it became evident to us that we should have to add a Roofing and Siding Department to our mills; if for no other reason than as a matter of convenience to the large number of patrons who wished to make up short carlots of galvanized sheets by adding the necessary tonnage of galvanized and painted roofing and siding.

We knew that there was not a great deal of profit in roofing, and that there *was* a great deal of dishonesty in weights and gauges. We knew that our galvanized sheets were far superior to the galvanized sheets that were commonly put into roofing and siding, and that it would be some time before the public could be educated up to the high standard that we were going to set.

But we had only one grade of galvanized sheet—the perfect, flawless, full-weight, basic open hearth sheet—and our patrons would have to buy and pay for that grade or go elsewhere. Our Roofing Department was therefore equipped with the best appliances the art had developed, and the same rigid rules of inspection and rejection that applied to all other departments were put in force here.

The result was a product of which we were and are extremely proud.

And, much to our surprise and gratification, we found that the buying public greeted our roofing and siding "with welcome arms"—and that we had really entered the field at the "psychological moment" when the cheapening process had reduced the average market product to so low a standard that honest roofers and dealers in roofing, disgusted with steel, were seeking for substitutes.

IMPORTANCE OF OPEN HEARTH

Just a word of warning in this connection: Never buy or use anything but Basic Open Hearth Steel for outdoor purposes or for a place indoors or out where gases or fumes abound.

A Bessemer Sheet Steel Roof is not worth the cost of putting on, because Bessemer is likely to rot and rust in a single season. Indeed, if the steel makers themselves had known as much about the frailties of Bessemer steel as they do now, they would never have so much as attempted to offer it to the public in the shape of steel for outdoor use.

Unfortunately, the Bessemer process is cheaper than the Open Hearth, so that steel makers still use it in making sheet bars. So much so that eighty per cent of the roofing in the open market today is Bessemer roofing.

In this connection let us drop a casual hint that it will pay anyone contemplating the purchase of any considerable tonnage of sheets for roofing, siding or other purposes to employ a chemist to analyze those offered, and to compare them chemically and physically with Inland Open Hearth Sheets.

THE END

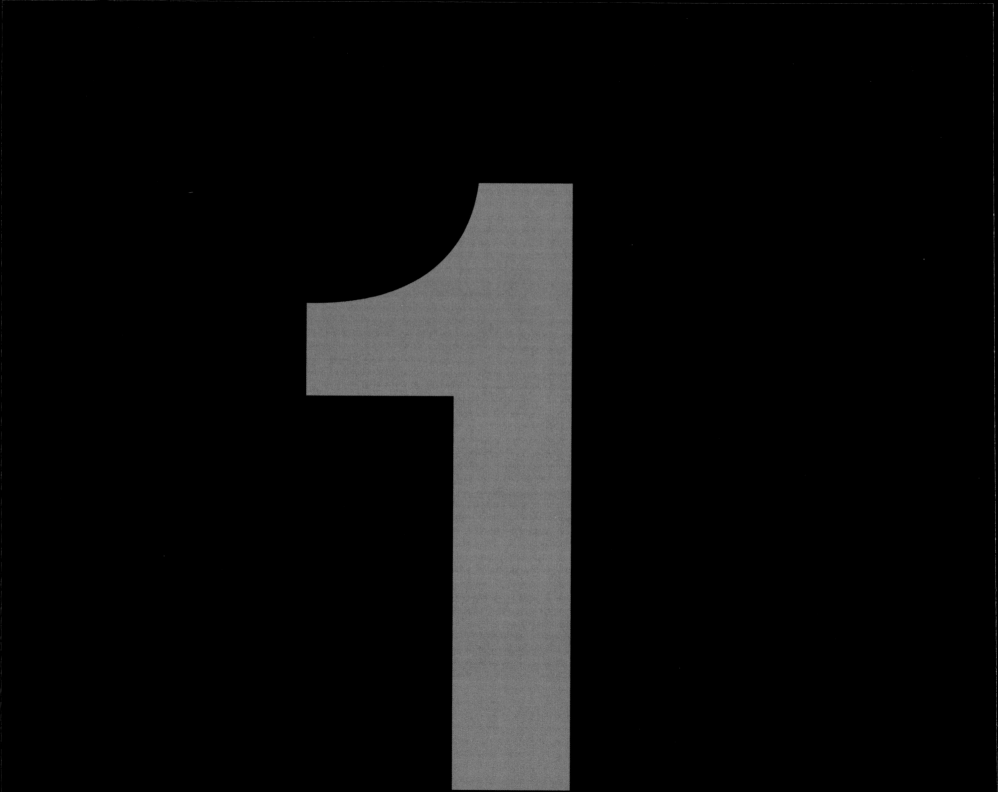

BUILDING THE
STEEL MILLS

Figure 1.1. Excavation for an open hearth furnace. August 3, 1906. U.S. Steel Gary Works.

Figure 1.2. Bridge at main entrance to plant looking toward site of main office. July 21, 1906. U.S. Steel Gary Works.

Figure 1.3.
Site of blast furnace no. 12.
July 17, 1906. U.S. Steel
Gary Works.

Figure 1.4.
Foundation of blast furnace
no. 12 and cast house. October 3,
1906. U.S. Steel Gary Works.

No. 135, MARCH 15-07. STOVES OF FURNACES Nos. 11 & 12.

Figure 1.5. Stoves of furnaces nos. 11 and 12. March 15, 1907. U.S. Steel Gary Works.

Figure 1.6. Blast furnace no. 9 and Stoves nos. 9 and 10. February 15, 1907. U.S. Steel Gary Works.

Figure 1.7.
Blast furnaces and Stoves nos. 9 and 10. April 3, 1907. U.S. Steel Gary Works.

Figure 1.8.
Stoves and furnaces nos. 9 and 10. June 17, 1907. U.S. Steel Gary Works.

Figure 1.9. Furnaces and stoves nos. 7 and 8. March 12, 1909. U.S. Steel Gary Works.

Figure 1.10. *(left)*
Blast furnaces. View from yard looking northeast at front side of blast furnace. April 30, 1913. U.S. Steel Gary Works.

Figure 1.11. *(below)*
Dump. Cinder and low level tracks; also Great Lakes stone and sand stock piles. Temp. 8°. Clear. February 3, 1916. Inland Steel Company Indiana Harbor Works.

Figure 1.12. View showing tug *H.C. Wild* breaking up ice floes. Temp. 20°. Clear. February 15, 1916. Inland Steel Company Indiana Harbor Works.

Figure 1.13.
Open hearth. 10,634 Cu. Yd. concrete run to date. Temp. 54°. Cloudy. March 31, 1916. Inland Steel Company Indiana Harbor Works.

Figure 1.14.
Blast furnace no. 3. Erecting first section of hearth jacket. Temp. 45°. Cloudy. May 2, 1916. Inland Steel Company Indiana Harbor Works.

Figure 1.15. *(facing)* View at pump station showing bricklayers starting brickwork. October 23, 1916. Inland Steel Company Indiana Harbor Works.

Figure 1.16. *(above)* View of Driver no. 65 with specially constructed leads driving a 95 ft. pile. March 20, 1917. Inland Steel Company Indiana Harbor Works.

Figure 1.17. View of ore-field extension showing progress of work on piles—driver excavation and concreting on dock unloader walls and west bridge wall. May 29, 1917. Inland Steel Company Indiana Harbor Works.

Figure 1.18.
Stoves of furnaces nos. 9 and 10.
Skip tank no. 9 and ore bins—
foundation. January 17, 1907.
U.S. Steel Gary Works.

Figure 1.19.
Furnace no. 9. August 2, 1907.
U.S. Steel Gary Works.

Figure 1.20. *(above right)*
Furnace no. 9. Cast house. August 20, 1907.
U.S. Steel Gary Works.

Figure 1.21. *(above left)*
Stoves and Furnaces nos. 9 and 10.
September 25, 1907. U.S. Steel Gary Works.

Figure 1.22. Building sewer from south. July 21, 1906. U.S. Steel Gary Works.

Figure 1.23. Opening channel. May 2, 1907. U.S. Steel Gary Works.

Figure 1.24. Panorama slip and turning basin from the south, showing north and northeast.
Plates 1–3. November 10, 1908. U.S. Steel Gary Works.

Figure 1.25.
Slip and harbor, under construction looking north. October 8, 1907. U.S. Steel Gary Works.

Figure 1.26.
Blast furnace trestle from B. & O. tracks. September 10, 1907. U.S. Steel Gary Works.

Figure 1.27.
Ore unloaders. September 10, 1907.
U.S. Steel Gary Works.

Figure 1.28.
Ore bins. September 25, 1907.
U.S. Steel Gary Works.

Figure 1.33. Bird's-eye view of work on ore-field extension showing progress on bridge walls, unloader walls, dock, and coal bunker. June 8, 1917. Inland Steel Company Indiana Harbor Works.

Figure 1.34. View at ore-field ext. showing progress of work on tunnel over conveyer A, coal bins, bridge walls, and highline trestle piers. Also forms for second section of coal bins. July 7, 1917. Inland Steel Company Indiana Harbor Works.

Figure 1.35. *(above)*
View showing steel for blast furnace highline extension unloaded and piers ready for steel erection. Also shows progress of work on coal bunkers. July 28, 1917. Inland Steel Company Indiana Harbor Works.

Figure 1.36. *(left)*
View at blast furnace highline showing progress of work on steel structure and brick retaining wall. September 1, 1917. Inland Steel Company Indiana Harbor Works.

Figure 1.37. Construction of no. 2 open hearth buildings. Photographer: Hedelius. October 7, 1937. Inland Steel Company Indiana Harbor Works.

No 977. JAN. 20. 10.
COKE OVENS BATTERY
#1 FROM EAST END.

Figure 1.38. Coke ovens battery no. 1 from east end. January 20, 1910. U.S. Steel Gary Works.

No 504. MAY 23.08. FURNACE No 6.

Figure 1.39. Furnace no. 6. May 23, 1908. U.S. Steel Gary Works.

No. 502 MAY 23-08. Stove Foundation 7&8.

Figure 1.40.
Stove foundation 7
and 8. May 23, 1908.
U.S. Steel Gary Works.

Figure 1.41. Plant no. 2—blast furnace no. 4—foundation brick work. July 21, 1925. Inland Steel Company Indiana Harbor Works.

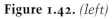

Figure 1.42. *(left)*
Blast furnace no. 4—stoves and A. C. station no. 2—erection. August 24, 1925. Inland Steel Company Indiana Harbor Works.

Figure 1.43. *(below)*
View at blast furnace no. 3 showing resumption of work on blast furnace after a delay of about one month waiting for furnace top. First sheet raised and in place. Also showing progress on dust catcher. October 23, 1916.
Inland Steel Company Indiana Harbor Works.

Figure 1.44. Hot blast mains to stove no. 9. May 17, 1907. U.S. Steel Gary Works.

Figure 1.45. *(left)*
Blast furnace no. 4—furnace top, erection. April 6, 1926. Inland Steel Company Indiana Harbor Works.

Figure 1.46. *(below)*
Blast furnace no. 4 and stoves—progress of erection. October 13, 1925. Inland Steel Company Indiana Harbor Works.

Figure 1.47.
Bird's-eye view showing progress on mill buildings also showing soaking pit stacks erected. August 22, 1916. Inland Steel Company Indiana Harbor Works.

Figure 1.48.
Interior blowing engine house to furnaces 5 to 8. February 25, 1910. U.S. Steel Gary Works.

Figure 1.49. View showing progress on new round house. Brickwork almost finished. February 23, 1917. Inland Steel Company Indiana Harbor Works.

Figure 1.50. Bird's-eye view of mill buildings and roll shop also showing progress of work at gas house. January 6, 1917. Inland Steel Company Indiana Harbor Works.

Figure 1.51. View showing progress of steel erection. Extension to blast furnace blowing engine room. August 30, 1918. Inland Steel Company Indiana Harbor Works.

Figure 1.52. Bird's-eye view showing open hearth building, soaking pit B, foundations for finishing mills, and cut for intake lines. Temp. 68°. May 9, 1916. Inland Steel Company Indiana Harbor Works.

Figure 1.53. Slab mill—looking west from roller table toward rolls.
February 28, 1914. U.S. Steel Gary Works.

Figure 1.54. Ore-field extension showing conveyer system used in removing excavation, and method of flushing it into place for backfill. June 18, 1917. Inland Steel Company Indiana Harbor Works.

Figure 1.55. Detail view at coal bunker showing men at work placing reinforcing iron. June 18, 1917. Inland Steel Company Indiana Harbor Works.

Figure 1.56. Central pumping station. View along east property line showing progress of work on new intake flume. April 29, 1920. Inland Steel Company Indiana Harbor Works.

Figure 1.57. View showing hopper bell for blast furnace being machined on new boring mill. December 28, 1918. Inland Steel Company Indiana Harbor Works.

Figure 1.58. View at scrap yard extension showing no. 8 crane and traveler hoisting crane girder for 97-ft. span. Taken a few seconds before cable on no. 8 crane parted, dropping girder to ground. July 13, 1917. Inland Steel Company Indiana Harbor Works.

Figure 1.59. *(left)*
Plant no. 2—blast furnace no. 4—drainage pit and site for highline and ore-field extension. March 17, 1925. Inland Steel Company Indiana Harbor Works.

Figure 1.60. *(below)*
Blast Furnace no. 4—skip pit. Sheet steel piling driven. August 11, 1925. Inland Steel Company Indiana Harbor Works.

Figure 1.61. 24″ billet and sheet bar mill, plant no. 1. Electrification. September 6, 1926. Inland Steel Company Indiana Harbor Works.

Figure 1.62. *(left)*
Machine shop.
September 25, 1907.
U.S. Steel Gary Works.

Figure 1.63. *(below)*
Looking south through 32"
mill showing
mixer working on
32" mill foundation.
August 12, 1916.
Inland Steel Company
Indiana Harbor Works.

Figure 1.64. Looking south on open hearth charging floor showing bricklayers working on open hearth furnaces nos. 18 and 19. August 22, 1916. Inland Steel Company Indiana Harbor Works.

Figure 1.65. View showing armatures of the largest and the smallest motors operated by Inland Steel Co. in the manufacture of steel. 1916. Inland Steel Company Indiana Harbor Works.

Figure 1.66. No. 1 strip mill—hot bed and tables. Looking from column E-51 toward columns D-46 and D-10. November 19, 1931. Inland Steel Company Indiana Harbor Works.

Figure 1.67. General office building. May 17, 1907. U.S. Steel Gary Works.

Figure 1.68. Side view of main office. August 30, 1917. U.S. Steel Gary Works.

Figure 1.69. Inland Steel Co. employment office. n.d. Inland Steel Company
Indiana Harbor Works.

Figure 1.70. Inland Steel Co. office building. January 6, 1930. Photographer: Fred J. Mimkes. Inland Steel Company Indiana Harbor Works.

THE PRODUCTION OF STEEL

Figure 2.1. *(above)*
Ore boats entering and leaving harbor. July 28, 1922.
U.S. Steel Gary Works.

Figure 2.2. *(left)*
U.S. Steel unloaders. 1941. U.S. Steel Gary Works.

Figure 2.3. Steamer, *Benjamin F. Fairless.* n.d. U.S. Steel Gary Works.

Figure 2.4. *(all views)* Mill from north balcony of hospital. February 4, 1912.
U.S. Steel Gary Works.

Figure 2.5. Interior blowing engine house to furnaces nos. 5 to 8 from north end. June 17, 1909. U.S. Steel Gary Works.

Figure 2.6.
View in Benzyl building. n.d.
Inland Steel Company Indiana
Harbor Works.

Figure 2.7.
Battery No. 6 coke ovens.
December 2, 1911. U.S. Steel
Gary Works.

Figure 2.8. Coke ovens. West coal bridge. December 28, 1913. U.S. Steel Gary Works.

Figure 2.9.
Coke ovens. Coal Handling Department—general view of buildings looking west from no. 1 coal bin. September 25, 1913. U.S. Steel Gary Works.

Figure 2.10.
Pusher side nos. 4 and 5 batteries, coke plant. 1920s. Inland Steel Company Indiana Harbor Works.

Figure 2.11. Coke plant shipping docks and storage tanks. July 21, 1916. U.S. Steel Gary Works.

Figure 2.12. View on no. 2 coal bridge showing bucket digging coal. August 30, 1917. Inland Steel Company Indiana Harbor Works.

Figure 2.13.
Kirk Yard, looking northeast at cinder pit. January 1, 1913. U.S. Steel Gary Works.

Figure 2.14.
Blast furnaces, looking north from northwest bridge at back of furnaces. October 16, 1917. U.S. Steel Gary Works.

Figure 2.15. Blast furnaces—transfer car no. 4. n.d. Inland Steel Company Indiana Harbor Works.

Figure 2.16. Blast furnace. View from middle platform over west track of no. 1 ore bridge looking northwest toward back side of blast furnace. April 30, 1913. U.S. Steel Gary Works.

Figure 2.17. Blast furnace, two ore bridges, pockets, and transfer car opposite no. 3 blast furnace. October 13, 1917. U.S. Steel Gary Works.

Nº 798. JUNE 5. 09. DUST CATCHERS & DOWN COMERS FURNACES 5 & 6.

Figure 2.18. *(facing, above)* Ore docks, looking north from east end of ore bridge no. 1. November 4, 1917. U.S. Steel Gary Works.

Figure 2.19. *(facing, below)* Dust catchers and down comers of furnaces nos. 5 and 6. June 5, 1909. U.S. Steel Gary Works.

Figure 2.20. *(above)* Plant no. 2—blast furnaces—limestone yard. June 12, 1923. Inland Steel Company Indiana Harbor Works.

Figure 2.21. No. 1 converter and jack car looking east. June 26, 1917. U.S. Steel Gary Works.

Figure 2.22. Three-quarters view of car for transferring iron ladle. July 10, 1913. U.S. Steel Gary Works.

No 892. SEP.23.09.
GAS MAINS. FURNACES
5 & 6. STOVES 5 & 6.

Figure 2.23. *(facing)* Gas mains furnace and stoves nos. 5 and 6. n.d. U.S. Steel Gary Works.

Figure 2.24. *(above)* View of 32" mill motor after turning over for the first time. December 29, 1916. Inland Steel Company Indiana Harbor Works.

Figure 2.25. *(left)*
Blast furnace no. 4—furnace and cast house, furnace operating. May 4, 1926. Inland Steel Company Indiana Harbor Works.

Figure 2.26. *(facing)*
No. 3 open hearth shop. Pugh ladle, special refractory lined standard gauge railroad car pouring pig iron from blast furnaces into small ladle at no. 3 open hearth shop. Ladle will in turn pour into bath of open hearth furnace. January, 1953. Photographer: R. M. Moore. Inland Steel Company Indiana Harbor Works.

Figure 2.27. No. 2 open hearth mixer pouring. June 23, 1917. U.S. Steel Gary Works.

Figure 2.28. View showing 150-ton open hearth crane lifting a test load of 200 tons. August 22, 1916. Inland Steel Company Indiana Harbor Works.

Figure 2.29. *(left)*
Open hearth no. 4 end view of cars of tin scrap with magnet holding load of scrap above car. April 23, 1912. U.S. Steel Gary Works.

Figure 2.30. *(facing)*
Section of scrap and nine buggies at no. 1 open hearth April 19, 1912. U.S. Steel Gary Works.

Figure 2.31. *(above)* No. 3 open hearth. Sampling heat of molten steel: *Left to Right:* (unidentified), 23357 with killing aluminum wire in hand; John Aumick, 23149, holding test ladle. George Lundie, plant safety, looks on. October 12, 1954. Photographer: Torkel Korling. Inland Steel Company Indiana Harbor Works.

Figure 2.32. *(facing)* Open hearth no. 4 charging side. June 5, 1909. U.S. Steel Gary Works.

Figure 2.33. Ingots. Optical pyrometer testing at pouring of ingot molds. January 1941. Photographer: Kaufmann & Fabry. Inland Steel Company Indiana Harbor Works.

Figure 2.34. Pouring molten steel with slag runoff. n.d. U.S. Steel Gary Works.

Figure 2.35. Pouring ingots. 1943. Inland Steel Company Indiana Harbor Works.

Figure 2.36. New Inland narrow gauge locomotive no. 15 pulling first heat of thirteen ingots from new open hearth plant no. 2. August 23, 1916. Inland Steel Company Indiana Harbor Works.

Figure 2.37. No. 1 stripper. August 24, 1919. U.S. Steel Gary Works.

Figure 2.38. Soaking pit crane handling ingots. June 5, 1909. U.S. Steel Gary Works.

Figure 2.39. *(above)*
North stripper first two ingots poured for slab mill. June 16, 1914.
U.S. Steel Gary Works.

Figure 2.40. *(facing)* View in 40" mill taken while rolling
first ingot. March 24, 1917. Inland Steel Company Indiana
Harbor Works.

Figure 2.41. 76" Hot strip mill. n.d. Inland Steel Company Indiana Harbor Works.

Figure 2.42. Interior rail mill shears. June 5, 1909. U.S. Steel Gary Works.

Figure 2.43. *(facing)* Axle mill steam hammer. July 27, 1927. U.S. Steel Gary Works.

Figure 2.44. *(above)* Semi-finished forms. Conveyor at 46" mill takes slabs to storage.
n.d. Photographer: Kaufmann & Fabry. Inland Steel Company Indiana Harbor Works.

Figure 2.45. *(facing)* Sheet (pack) mills. Obsolete method of pack rolling sheets. 1933. Photographer: Shigeta Wright. Inland Steel Company Indiana Harbor Works.

Figure 2.46. *(above)* 76″ Continuous strip mill. Finishing stands of 76″ hot strip. n.d. Photographer: Kaufmann & Fabry. Inland Steel Company Indiana Harbor Works.

Figure 2.47. Pickling. Steel sheet gets its silvery surface by immersion in an acid solution that removes hot mill scale—a process know as "pickling." Steel sheet is shown entering continuous pickling line. 1936. Photographer: Kaufmann & Fabry. Inland Steel Company Indiana Harbor Works.

Figure 2.48. Big milling machine in machine shop. November 10, 1912. U.S. Steel Gary Works.

Figure 2.49. *(above)* Galvanizing. Corrugating galvanized sheets at plant no. 1. February 20, 1937. Inland Steel Company Indiana Harbor Works.

Figure 2.50. *(facing)* Open hearth project no. 3. Before a heavy steel plant addition can be built, the ground must be tested to determine its resistance to the enormous weights. This test load of 600 tons of ingot rests on bearing piles whose settling, if any, is checked by surveyors' transits. n.d. Photographer: Adolph Pressler. Inland Steel Company Indiana Harbor Works.

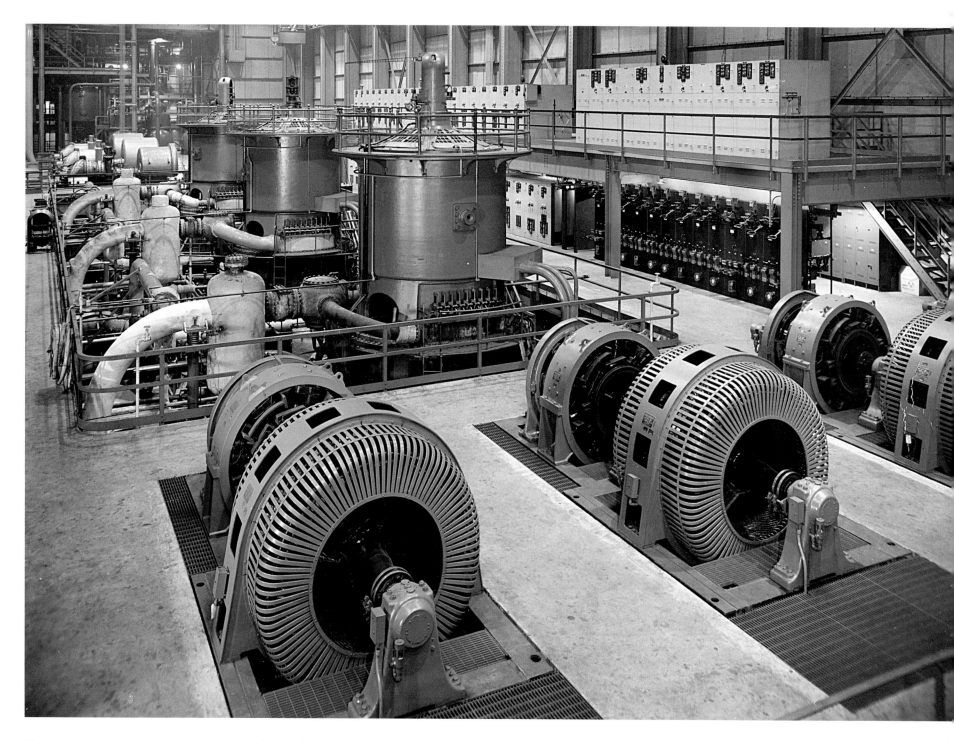

Figure 2.51. D. P. C. plant—Indiana Harbor, Indiana. Plancor 266. Power house looking west showing generators and blowers. Switch board. Corrugating galvanized sheets at plant no. 1. February 19, 1944. Inland Steel Company Indiana Harbor Works.

Figure 2.52.
D. P. C. plant—Indiana Harbor.
Plancor 266. View of top of furnace
A looking north. February 19,
1944. Inland Steel Company
Indiana Harbor Works.5, 1913.
U.S. Steel Gary Works.

Figure 2.53. *(facing)* First heat at no. 4 basic oxygen furnace shop. July 24, 1966. Inland Steel Company Indiana Harbor Works.

Figure 2.54. *(above)* Inland foundry. 1970s. Inland Steel Company Indiana Harbor Works.

Figure 2.55. Open hearth. n.d. U.S. Steel Gary Works.

Figure 2.56. Molten slag pouring. n.d. U.S. Steel Gary Works.

Figure 2.57. Steel rolls ready for shipment. n.d. Inland Steel Company Indiana Harbor Works.

3

STEEL
COMMUNITIES

Figure 3.1. Shacks along river—view 1. March 15, 1907. U.S. Steel Gary Works.

Figure 3.2. View of the ship harbor with squatters shack in foreground and a wooden steamboat in the background tied to the dock which eventually became Inland Steel Co. property. On the dock can be seen piles of railroad ties. n.d. Inland Steel Company Indiana Harbor Works.

Figure 3.3. *Top:* South Bay Hotel, Indiana Harbor, with Inland blast furnace at right, ca. 1907. *Bottom:* Looking east of South Bay Hotel.at home of General Superintendent John Stephens, n.d. Inland Steel Company Indiana Harbor Works.

Indiana Harbor,Ind.

Figure 3.4. Intersection of 5th and Broadway. July 1, 1907. U.S. Steel Gary Works.

Figure 3.5. Housing construction, Harrison north from 7th Avenue. December 19, 1906.
U.S. Steel Gary Works.

Figure 3.6. Harrison Street looking north from 8th Avenue. Town site. January 17, 1907. U.S. Steel Gary Works.

Figure 3.7. Looking west on 141st Street from Short Street. September 14, 1920. Inland Steel Company Indiana Harbor Works.

Figure 3.8. View looking east on 140th Place from Butternut Street. November 27, 1920. Inland Steel Company Indiana Harbor Works.

Figure 3.9. *(above)* Lake Shore and Michigan Southern depot, n.d.
Inland Steel Company Indiana Harbor Works.

Figure 3.10. *(facing)* Harbor Hotel, built in 1901.
Inland Steel Company Indiana Harbor Works.

Figure 3.11. Michigan Avenue East, Indiana Harbor, Indiana. n.d. Inland Steel Company Indiana Harbor Works.

Figure 3.12. Union Depot L.S. & M.S. and B.&O. Railways. July 12, 1910. U.S. Steel Gary Works.

Figure 3.13. 5th Avenue east from Washington Street across Broadway. November 10, 1908. U.S. Steel Gary Works.

Figure 3.14. Broadway north from 7th Avenue. November 19, 1907. U.S. Steel Gary Works.

Figure 3.15. Fifth Avenue west from Massachusetts Street, across Broadway. November 10, 1908. U.S. Steel Gary Works.

Figure 3.16. Broadway north from 8th Avenue. November 6, 1908. U.S. Steel Gary Works.

Figure 3.17. Broadway looking North from south of 6th Avenue. July 29, 1913. U.S. Steel Gary Works.

Figure 3.18. Broadway looking north from south of Fifth Avenue. June 6, 1913. U.S. Steel Gary Works.

Figure 3.19. General view—city water tower and pumping station from public park.
July 14, 1910. U.S. Steel Gary Works.

Figure 3.20. City church building. April 21, 1931. U.S. Steel Gary Works.

Figure 3.21. *Top:* View of Indiana Harbor looking east from an elevated point in the vicinity of the Inland Steel Company plant entrance. The street on the right is Block Avenue; extreme left is the L.S. & M.S. depot, then the South Bay Hotel. The large building on the right of Block Avenue is the Harbor Hotel. 1903. *Bottom:* View of the west side of Michigan Avenue with the Harbor Hotel on the extreme right and the bank building on the extreme left. The building under construction is on the northwest corner of Michigan and Pennsylvania Avenues. August 27, 1904. Inland Steel Company Indiana Harbor Works.

Figure 3.22. *Top:* East from Michigan Avenue and L.S. & M.S. R. Taken from the L.S. & M.S. depot, in background are the tracks of the B&O Railroad. The building to the right was occupied by John H. McGrath, the first Open Hearth superintendent. The building to the left was called the Pavilion. There was a combination restaurant and bar on the main floor with dancing on the upper floor. A pier extended into the lake at this point and boats from Chicago, bringing passengers, would tie up the evening and make the return trip to Chicago when the Pavilion had closed. August 27, 1904. *Bottom:* West from Michigan Avenue and L.S. & M.S. R. View of the business district of Indiana Harbor in the center background. On the left is a building at the corner of Michigan and Commonwealth Avenue and on the right is the plant. August 27, 1904. Inland Steel Company Indiana Harbor Works.

Figure 3.23. *Above:* View showing progress of work on Inland Steel Co. Community Center. October 21, 1918.
Facing: View showing progress of work on Inland Steel Co. Community Center. November 25, 1918.
Inland Steel Company Indiana Harbor Works (both photos).

Figure 3.24. View showing central building nearly finished, Inland Steel Co. Community Center. December 5, 1918. Inland Steel Company Indiana Harbor Works.

Figure 3.25. Looking west from 141st and Catalpa Streets. April 21, 1920. Inland Steel Company Indiana Harbor Works.

Figure 3.26. Looking north on Butternut Street from 141st Street. June 24, 1920. Inland Steel Company Indiana Harbor Works.

Figure 3.27. Offices and camp. May 18, 1920. Inland Steel Company Indiana Harbor Works.

Figure 3.28. Girls in school. n.d. U.S. Steel Gary Works.

Figure 3.29. Emerson School. June 30, 1913. U.S. Steel Gary Works.

Figure 3.30. *(above facing)* Froebel School, 15th Avenue. June 6, 1913. U.S. Steel Gary Works.

Figure 3.31. *(below facing)* Jefferson School. n.d. U.S. Steel Gary Works.

Figure 3.32. *(above)* Students in auditorium. n.d. U.S. Steel Gary Works.

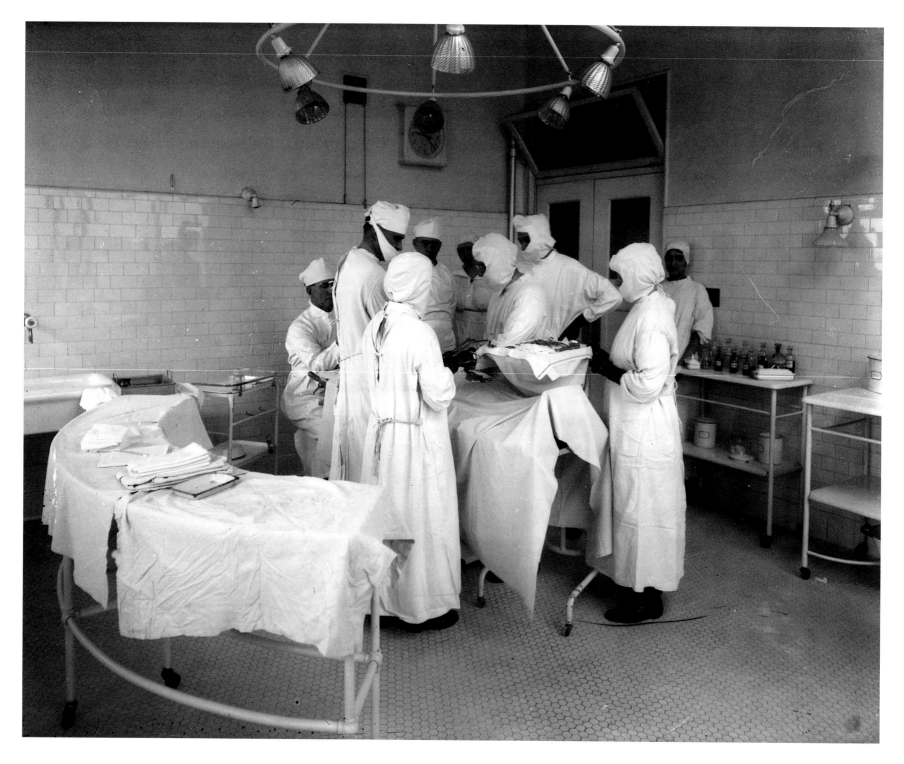

Figure 3.33. *(above)* View of group taken at Mercy Hospital. November 2, 1919. U.S. Steel Gary Works.

Figure 3.34. *(facing)* Musical group. n.d. U.S. Steel Gary Works.

Figure 3.35. *(above)* View looking southeast at 4th, 5th, 6th, and 7th cottages from west, showing Keeper's House in rear of 6th cottage. August 29, 1913. U.S. Steel Gary Works.

Figure 3.36. *(above facing)* City, looking north at Carolina Street from 14th Avenue. June 3, 1918. U.S. Steel Gary Works.

Figure 3.37. *(below facing)* Jackson Street north from 8th Avenue. November 6, 1908. U.S. Steel Gary Works.

Figure 3.38. House, 176 and 178 Ellsworth, style 241, Gary Land Company #34. August 18, 1915. U.S. Steel Gary Works.

Figure 3.39. City, garden at 555 Connecticut Street. August 17, 1917. U.S. Steel Gary Works.

Figure 3.40. 617 Jefferson Street, style N, Gary Land Company #56. August 18, 1915. U.S. Steel Gary Works.

Figure 3.41. House, 440 Marshall Street, style 242, Gary Land Company 333. August 18, 1915. U.S. Steel Gary Works.

Figure 3.42. House, 750 Delaware Street, style P, Gary Land Company 357. September 1, 1915. U.S. Steel Gary Works.

Figure 3.43. House, 636–44 Van Buren Street, styles B1, B2, B3, and B4, Gary Land Company #66.
August 19, 1915. U.S. Steel Gary Works.

Figure 3.44. House, 630 Jackson. Kirk residence, Gary Land Company #58. August 19, 1915. U.S. Steel Gary Works.

Figure 3.45. View looking south on Butternut Street from 140th Street. June 8, 1920. Inland Steel Company Indiana Harbor Works.

Figure 3.46. Looking south on Butternut Street from 140th Street. July 15, 1920. Inland Steel Company Indiana Harbor Works.

Figure 3.47. Looking south on Butternut Street from 141st Street. October 9, 1920. Inland Steel Company Indiana Harbor Works.

Figure 3.48. *(above)* View looking north on Butternut Street from house no. 28. November 27, 1920. Inland Steel Company Indiana Harbor Works.

Figure 3.49. *(facing)* Gary National Bank. 1931. U.S. Steel Gary Works.

Figure 3.50. Gary Silver Anniversary Parade. June 5, 1931. U.S. Steel Gary Works.

Figure 3.51. New building at Lake Front (Marquette) Park. October 1, 1924. U.S. Steel Gary Works.

Figure 3.52. View showing west side of Broadway from 7th Avenue. March 2, 1931. U.S. Steel Gary Works.

Figure 3.53. Gary Gateway. April 22, 1931. U.S. Steel Gary Works.

Figure 3.54. *(left)*
Father Marquette statue. June 27, 1932. U.S. Steel Gary Works.

Figure 3.55. *(above)*
Male chorus concert and show at Memorial Auditorium.
May 25, 1939. U.S. Steel Gary Works.

Figure 3.56. Male chorus concert and show at Memorial Auditorium. May 25, 1939.
U.S. Steel Gary Works.

**STEEL
PEOPLE**

Figure 4.1. *(facing)* Typical sheet mill crew. 1904. Inland Steel Company Indiana Harbor Works.

Figure 4.2. *(above)* No. 1 open hearth plant no. 1. 1—Jim Doherty, 2—Al Sirlin, 3—Galvin, 4—Mentzer, 5—Casey. 1904. Inland Steel Company Indiana Harbor Works.

Figure 4.3. Parade on Broadway after arrival of first ore boat. July 23, 1908. U.S. Steel Gary Works.

Figure 4.4. View under open hearth charging floor showing men at work setting Blair valves. June 30, 1916. Inland Steel Company Indiana Harbor Works.

Figure 4.5. *(above)* Safety record—1921. Taken north of Benzyl building. *Top Row:* Johnson, Gallistel, E. Ball, J. Farris, Dickinson, Tate, Leach, Mackin, Cowart, Nevius, Edwards, Van See, Patnode, Junglen, Bundy. *Bottom Row:* McMahon, H. Stein, Schottmueller, Tompkins, P. Donohue, Gardner, Ball, Crowder, Boardman, Rosenberg, Corbett, Seede, West. Inland Steel Company Indiana Harbor Works.

Figure 4.6. *(facing)* Bi-plane at Gary Works. n.d. U.S. Steel Gary Works.

Figure 4.7. Inland Steel Co. plant no. 2. Laboratory office. 1919.
Inland Steel Company Indiana Harbor Works.

Figure 4.8. View of employment office showing crowd. November 21, 1919.
U.S. Steel Gary Works.

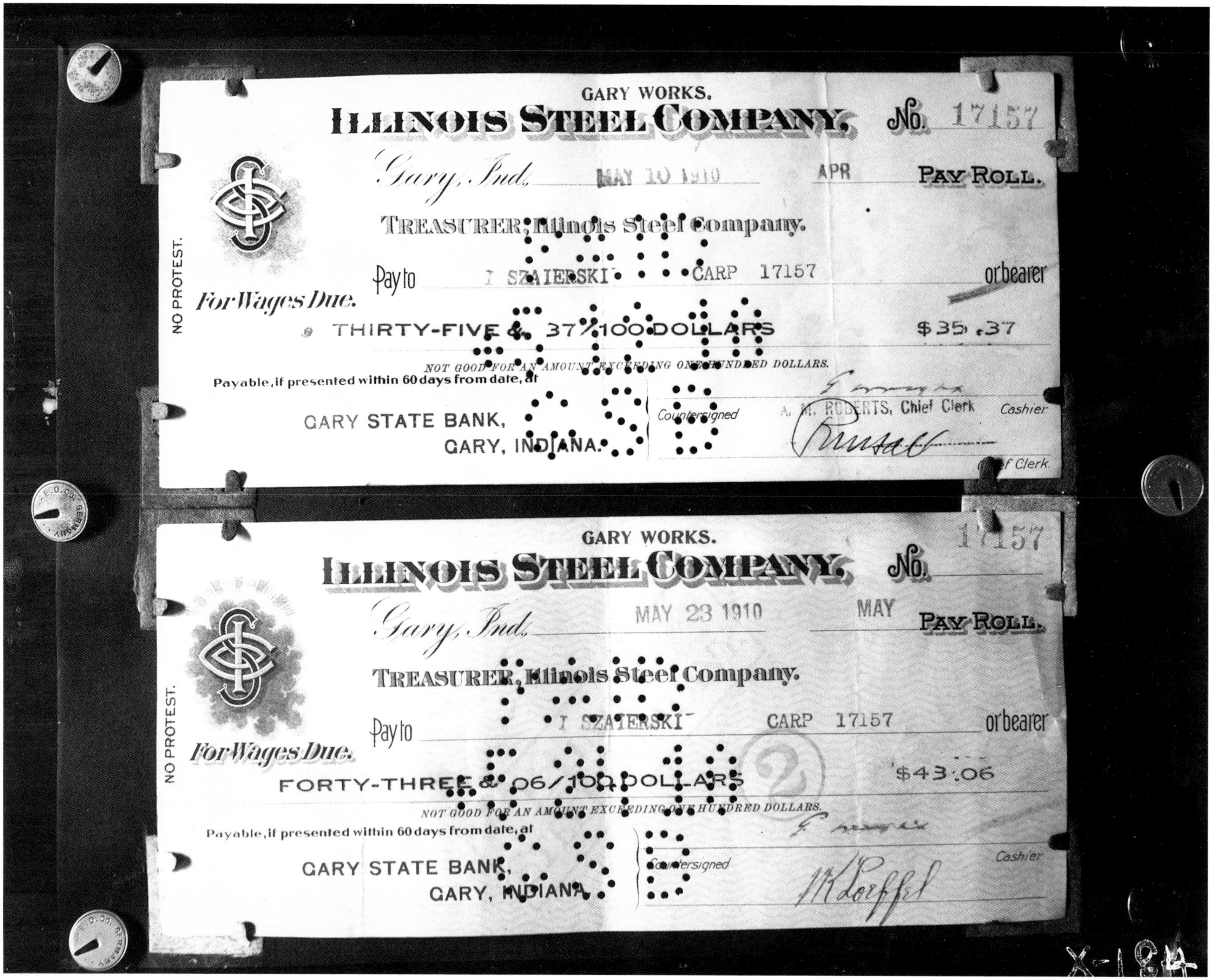

Figure 4.9. *(above)* Paycheck—Ignatz Szaierski. December 9, 1911. U.S. Steel Gary Works.

Figure 4.10. *(facing)* Blacksmith shop. Largest hook ever forged in blacksmith shop, weight 900 lbs. for open hearth ladle crane. April 23, 1913. U.S. Steel Gary Works.

4
HAMMERS MUST NOT
BEOPERATED FOR OR
BY ANY ONE NOT EMPLO
YED IN BLACKSMITH
SHOP
HANDS-OFF
18009

Figure 4.11. English class. April 14, 1921. U.S. Steel Gary Works.

Figure 4.12. Safety. Watch drawing at blast furnace department. May 3, 1920.
Inland Steel Company Indiana Harbor Works.

Figure 4.13. Locomotive No. 12, order dept., American Bridge Co., Gary Plant. June 24, 1918. U.S. Steel Gary Works.

Figure 4.14. View showing locomotive crane operating steam hammer on excavation for 600-ton hot metal mixer. Open hearth plant no. 2. October 10, 1918. Inland Steel Company Indiana Harbor Works.

Figure 4.15. Orefield extension. View showing diver going down to cut off bearing pile and sheeting on face of dock for 72" intake line. September 11, 1917. Inland Steel Company Indiana Harbor Works.

Figure 4.16. Group of electricians—plant no. 2. September 20, 1920.
Inland Steel Company Indiana Harbor Works.

Figure 4.17. Sheet mill plant no. 1. n.d. Photographer: Shigeta Wright.
Inland Steel Company Indiana Harbor Works.

Figure 4.18. H. B. Hubbard, superintendent, and Fred Spangler in the mold yard, plant no. 1 open hearth, with stripper building in the background. 1920s. Inland Steel Company Indiana Harbor Works.

Figure 4.19. Gary Works basketball team. February 5, 1920. U.S. Steel Gary Works.

Figure 4.20. Gary Works baseball team. September 14, 1912. U.S. Steel Gary Works.

Figure 4.21. Women's softball. 1945. Inland Steel Company Indiana Harbor Works.

Figure 4.22. Chemical lab track team, Gleason Park. September 6, 1917. U.S. Steel Gary Works.

Figure 4.23. A picture of the sheet bar yard, plant no. 1. This is the way the sheet bar came from the mill and was stored previous to shearing into bars. Bob Watson is pictured in the foreground. 1920. Inland Steel Company Indiana Harbor Works.

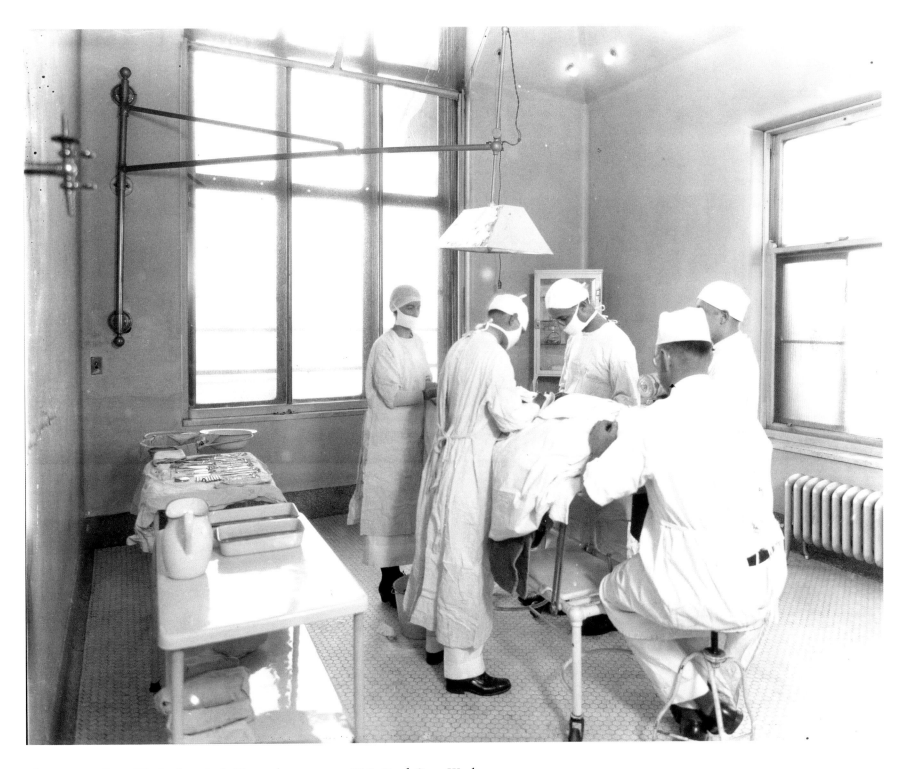

Figure 4.24. Gary Works hospital. November 11, 1925. U.S. Steel Gary Works.

Figure 4.25. Blast furnaces. View of lorry car and crew in blast furnace stock house. April 16, 1913. U.S. Steel Gary Works.

Figure 4.26. Excavation for no. 2 stack base, Springfield boiler house. Also method of supporting flue. May 26, 1920. Inland Steel Company Indiana Harbor Works.

Figure 4.27. Foundry, washhouse in active service. November 11, 1917. U.S. Steel Gary Works.

Figure 4.28. Axle mill. Bathhouse wash bowls. January 7, 1914. U.S. Steel Gary Works.

Figure 4.29. Plant restaurant—counter and waiter. May 1, 1918. U.S. Steel Gary Works.

Figure 4.30. Chemistry class. March 21, 1918. U.S. Steel Gary Works.

Figure 4.31.
Apprentice class at main office.
April 9, 1926. U.S. Steel Gary Works.

Figure 4.32.
Home guards, group of exempted
employees training under K. M. Burr.
September 15, 1918. U.S. Steel
Gary Works.

Figure 4.33. Views at tin mill, American Sheet and Tin Plate Co. January 28, 1921.
U.S. Steel Gary Works.

X-1642

Figure 4.34. *(above)* Stage at Goodfellow Club party at Broadway Theater.
December 24, 1917. U.S. Steel Gary Works.

Figure 4.35. *(facing)* City, Goodfellow Club Christmas celebration outside theater.
December 23, 1916. U.S. Steel Gary Works.

Figure 4.36. Truck drivers safety meeting. March 24, 1922. U.S. Steel Gary Works.

Figure 4.37. Bar mill employees. 1920s. Inland Steel Company Indiana Harbor Works.

Figure 4.38. Crew of merchant mill. April 8, 1913. U.S. Steel Gary Works.

Figure 4.39. Bathing beach—Lake Front Park (Marquette Park). July 1, 1921. U.S. Steel Gary Works.

Figure 4.40. View of Illinois Steel Company welfare station. July 9, 1921. U.S. Steel Gary Works.

Figure 4.41. Indians visiting plant. April 1, 1924. U.S. Steel Gary Works.

Figure 4.42. Hammond (Indiana) School System teachers inspecting Halden shear line in cold strip mill at the Inland Steel Company's Indiana Harbor Works. Photographer: R. M. Moore. October 1950. Inland Steel Company Indiana Harbor Works.

Figure 4.43.
Mr. Gleason and party in mills with
Queen Marie. December 8, 1926.
U.S. Steel Gary Works.

Figure 4.44. 1907 dedication of Inland Steel Company's first blast furnace was the responsibility of five-year-old Madeline Block, daughter of Inland founder Philip D. Block. Seventy-three years later (on Sept. 19, 1980) Mrs. Madeline Block Willner dedicated Inland's no. 7 furnace, the largest in the Western Hemisphere and most advanced technologically in the world. In its first campaign, Madeline no. 1 produced an average of 345 tons per day of pig iron for steelmaking, an hour's work or less for Madeline no. 7, which is rated at 7,000 to 10,000 tons per day. Inland Steel Company Indiana Harbor Works.

Figure 4.45. Madeline Block lighting blast furnace. April 4, 1912.
Inland Steel Company Indiana Harbor Works.

Figure 4.46.
Madeline furnace no. 5
dedication ceremony.
Left to right:
Madeline Block
Strauss, Geo. H. Jones,
L. E. Block, P. O. Block.
January 1939. Inland
Steel Company Indiana
Harbor Works.

Figure 4.47. Dedication of new blast furnace—The Inland Steel company's new no. 6 blast furnace was "blown in" Nov. 16 (Monday) at a special ceremony held in the Indiana Harbor plant. The button starting the furnace in operation was pressed by Mrs. Henry Straus (Madeline Block) of Glencoe, Ill., (with flowers), daughter of the late P. D. Block, one of the founders of the company and at the time of his death chairman of Inland's executive committee. At the microphone is Wilfred Sykes, Inland president, and to his left, front row, E. L. Ryerson, chairman of the board of directors. At extreme left is J. H. Walsh, vice-president in charge of operations at Indiana Harbor for Inland. November 16, 1942. Inland Steel Company Indiana Harbor Works.

Figure 4.48. Lighting ceremony, Madeline no. 7 blast furnace, Madeline Block Willner and Frank Kik. September 19, 1980. Inland Steel Company Indiana Harbor Works.

Figure 4.49. Superintendent J. W. Lees introducing Sailor Blake. June 21, 1918.
Inland Steel Company Indiana Harbor Works.

Figure 4.50. *(above)* Exhibit of Christmas gifts to soldiers from electric shop. December 17, 1917. U.S. Steel Gary Works.

Figure 4.51. *(facing)* View of open hearth flag pole showing man climbing up pole to unfurl flag. August 25, 1917. Inland Steel Company Indiana Harbor Works.

DO NOT DRIVE FASTER
DANGER-LOOK
NEBEZPECNO-DAJ
VESELY-VIGYAZ
OPAZNO-PAZITE
NIEBEZPECZENSTWO-

Figure 4.52. *(facing)* Dr. R. C. Hamilton, just before his return to work after military service. On the right of the picture is one of the danger signs with warnings in five different languages. n.d. Inland Steel Company Indiana Harbor Works.

Figure 4.53. *(above)* Flag raising at 14″ and 18″ mills. April 15, 1917. U.S. Steel Gary Works.

Figure 4.54. "To Every Good American Your Country Must Have Your Financial Help To Win This War. Bear Down And Buy All The Bonds You Can, This Is Your Duty." n.d. Photographer: R. M. Moore. Inland Steel Company Indiana Harbor Works.

Figure 4.55. Inland receives maritime "M" award. October 4, 1943. Photographer: R. M. Moore. Inland Steel Company Indiana Harbor Works.

Figure 4.56. Inland receives maritime "M" award. October 4, 1943. Photographer: Allison & Lighthall. Inland Steel Company Indiana Harbor Works.

Figure 4.57. Inland Steel at war. 1943. Inland Steel Company Indiana Harbor Works.

Figure 4.58. Female crane operator in foundry operation, electric shop supervision. 1943.
U.S. Steel Gary Works.

Figure 4.59. Blast furnaces. 1943. U.S. Steel Gary Works.

Figure 4.60. Crane operator. 1942. Inland Steel Company Indiana Harbor Works.

Figure 4.61. Power and fuel. 1943. U.S. Steel Gary Works.

Figure 4.62. (*above*) Wrench operator, blast furnace. 1943. U.S. Steel Gary Works.

Figure 4.63. (*facing*) Mrs. Kathrine Lemmons, flame cutting burner. 1942. U.S. Steel Gary Works.

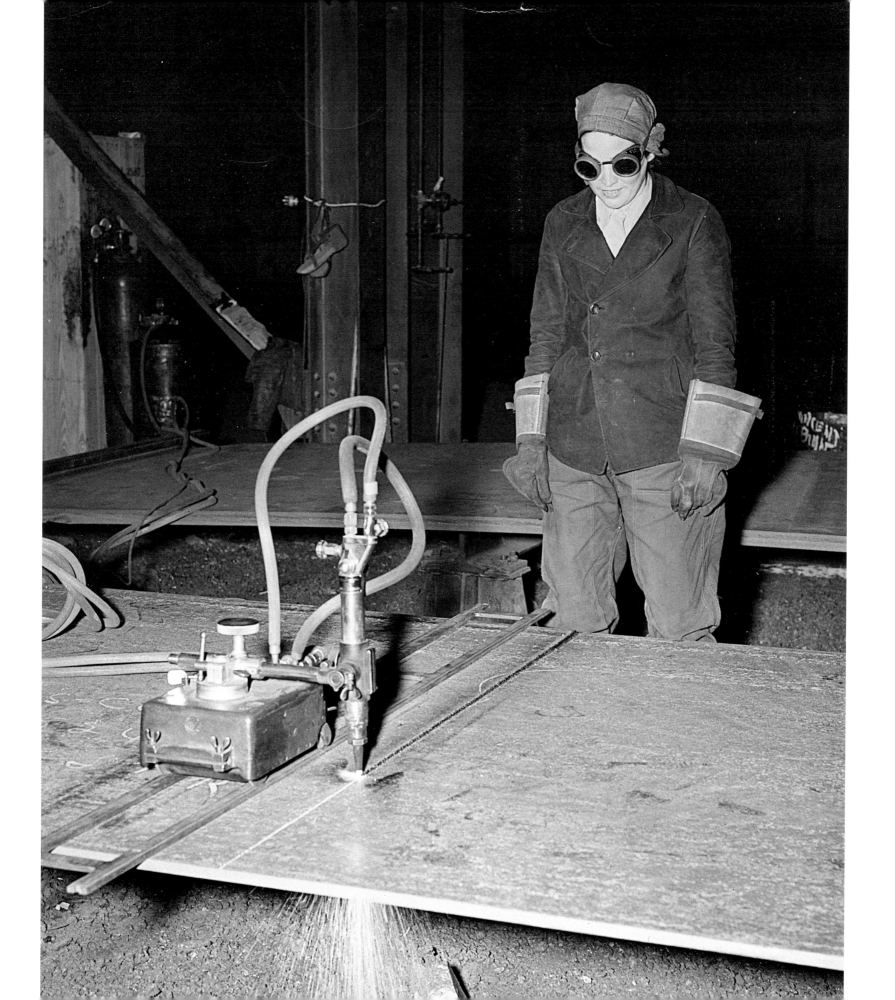

Figure 4.64. *(above)* Mrs. Betty Aitken—production control checker. 1942.
U.S. Steel Gary Works.

Figure 4.65. *(facing)* Tin mill—inspecting and sorting tin plate. n.d.
Inland Steel Company Indiana Harbor Works.

Figure 4.66. Inspection class. 1943. U.S. Steel Gary Works.

Figure 4.67. Billet mill—grinders. 1943. U.S. Steel Gary Works.

Figure 4.68.
Foundry. 1943.
U.S. Steel Gary Works.

Figure 4.69. James Cagney—war bonds drive. n.d. Inland Steel Company Indiana Harbor Works.

Figure 4.70. Scrap drive. Mr. F. Camandella, Roscoe Sopher—chairman of scrap drive, Ross Trester—mayor of Hobart, Paul Heuring—president of Lions Club; *Back row:* Wilbur Nicholas—1ˢᵗ Vice Pres., Dick Harkins—secretary, Bryon Findling—project committee. n.d. Inland Steel Company Indiana Harbor Works.

Figure 4.71. Scrap drive—autos. n.d. Inland Steel Company Indiana Harbor Works.

Figure 4.72. Scrap drive. Chicago Belt Railway Company's West Yard at clearing district, Chicago. Three of seven scrap locomotives and tenders are shown, together with now obsolete coal tipple. These items were contribution to the ferrous scrap drive; find made by McBride and Toggweiller, both of Republic Steel Corporation—Chicago sales office, on the local scrap committee, under John G. Mack, Jr., of Inland. December 27, 1951. Inland Steel Company Indiana Harbor Works.

Figure 4.73. Galvanized sheets. Matt Gambla, extra loader lifts Ti-Co, Inland's trade name for the new and improved product processed on the new line. 1951. Photographer: R. M. Moore. Inland Steel Company Indiana Harbor Works.

Figure 4.74. *(above)* Bolt and spike department. Joe Kirincic, 45, who is blind and yet is one of the most efficient "nutter ups" in the department. n.d. Photographer: Kaufmann & Fabry. Inland Steel Company Indiana Harbor Works.

Figure 4.75. *(facing)* Boats—P. D. Block. A crew member of the *Phillip D. Block* and his concertina. 1947. Photographer: R. M. Moore. Inland Steel Company Indiana Harbor Works.

Figure 4.76. Vintage picture of steelmakers leaving Indiana Harbor Works. n.d. Inland Steel Company Indiana Harbor Works.

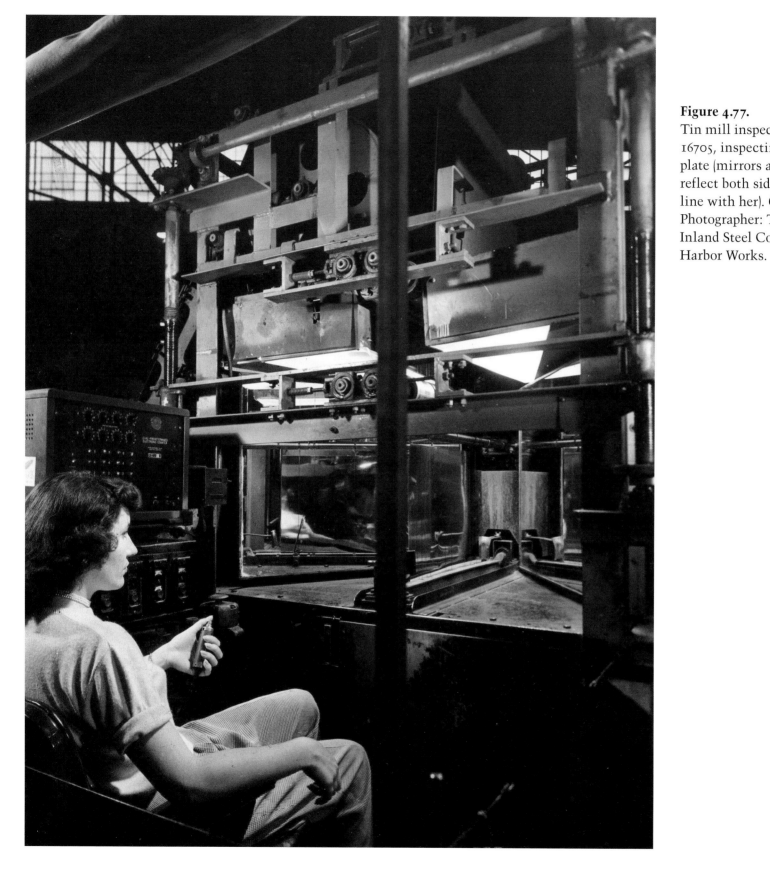

Figure 4.77.
Tin mill inspection. Nina Pecoraro, 16705, inspecting cut sheets of tin plate (mirrors at 45° to her vision reflect both sides of tin sheet in line with her). October 15, 1954. Photographer: Torkel Korling. Inland Steel Company Indiana Harbor Works.

Figure 4.78. Tin mill—banding tin rolls. June 1954. Inland Steel Company Indiana Harbor Works.

Figure 4.79.
Inland Steel Yard
Department worker,
September 1962.
Inland Steel Company,
Indiana Harbor Works.

Stephen G. McShane

is the archivist/curator of the Calumet Regional Archives at Indiana University Northwest's library, and editor (with Ronald D. Cohen) of *Moonlight in Duneland* (Indiana University Press, 1998).

Gary S. Wilk

is an associate professor of the fine arts department at Indiana University Northwest.